VALLEY PARK COMMUNITY
320 Benton St.
Valley Park, MO 63088

D0811651

VALLEY PARK COMMUNITY LIBRARY
320 Benton St.
Valley Park, MO 63088

FIRST BATTLE OF THE MARNE

GETTYSBURG

HASTINGS

MARATHON

MIDWAY

NORMANDY

SARATOGA

TENOCHTITLAN

TET OFFENSIVE

WATERLOO

4-24-03

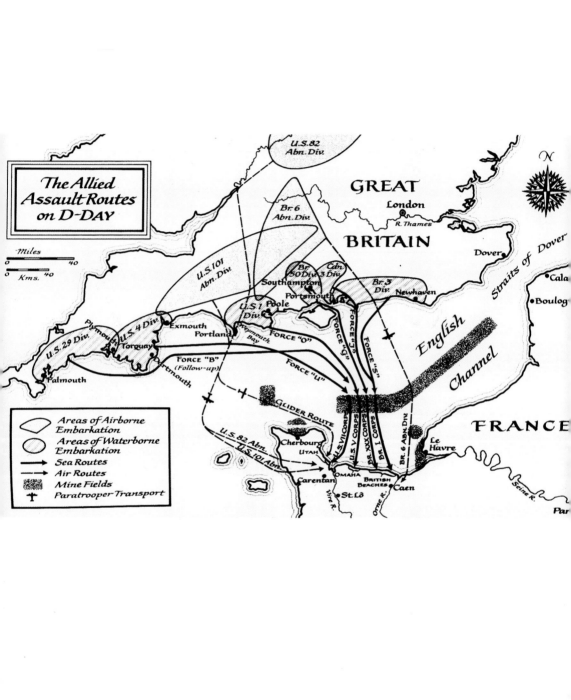

The Allied Assault Routes on D-DAY

BATTLES
THAT CHANGED THE WORLD

NORMANDY

EARLE RICE JR.

CHELSEA HOUSE PUBLISHERS
PHILADELPHIA

Frontispiece: This map shows the assault routes used by the Allies on D Day. The whole south of England turned into a supply depot to provide manpower, transportation, supplies, and weaponry to support the huge invasion.

CHELSEA HOUSE PUBLISHERS

EDITOR IN CHIEF Sally Cheney
DIRECTOR OF PRODUCTION Kim Shinners
CREATIVE MANAGER Takeshi Takahashi
MANUFACTURING MANAGER Diann Grasse

STAFF FOR NORMANDY

EDITOR Lee Marcott
ASSOCIATE EDITOR Bill Conn
PICTURE RESEARCHER Patricia Burns
PRODUCTION ASSISTANT Jaimie Winkler
SERIES AND COVER DESIGNER Keith Trego
LAYOUT 21st Century Publishing and Communications, Inc.

©2002 by Chelsea House Publishers,
a subsidiary of Haights Cross Communications.
All rights reserved. Printed and bound in the United States of America.

http://www.chelseahouse.com

First Printing

1 3 5 7 9 8 6 4 2

Library of Congress Cataloging-in-Publication Data

Rice, Earle.
   Normandy / Earle Rice, Jr.
      p. cm. — (Battles that changed the world)
Includes bibliographical references and index.
   ISBN 0-7910-6687-8 — ISBN 0-7910-7109-X (pbk.)
 1. World War, 1939-1945—Campaigns—France—Normandy—Juvenile literature.
2. Normandy (France)—History, Military—Juvenile literature. I. Title. II. Series.
D756.5.N6 R52 2002
940.54'2142—dc21

                                                    2002002135

TABLE OF CONTENTS

Planning for the Allied invasion at Normandy began as early as 1941. But in early June 1944, the weather forecast threatened to wreck havoc with the years of preparation. The decision whether to proceed with the invasion was ultimately up to General Dwight Eisenhower, Supreme Allied Commander (front row, center), shown here at his London Headquarters with other members of the Supreme Command Allied Expedition Force, January 1944.

The Long Wait Ends

Almighty God—Our sons, pride of our nation, this day have set upon a mighty endeavor, a struggle to preserve our Republic, our religion, and our civilization and to set free a suffering humanity . . .

—President Franklin D. Roosevelt,
in his statement on D Day, June 6, 1944
(quoted in Charles B. MacDonald,
The Mighty Endeavor)

On the night of June 4, 1944—a blustery night fit only for the hardiest of souls—14 high-ranking Allied officers gathered in the mess room of Southwick House at the request of their commander. Tension pervaded the atmosphere in General Dwight D. "Ike" Eisenhower's temporary Supreme Headquarters Allied Expeditionary Force (SHAEF) near Portsmouth, England. The Allied invasion of Normandy in World War II—the greatest seaborne operation the world has ever known—had been scheduled to begin at dawn on June 5, weather permitting. But at 9:30 P.M. on June 3, Royal Air Force Group captain John M. Stagg, Eisenhower's chief meteorologist, had reported that the forecast for the British Isles and the North Atlantic was "very disturbed and complex."

Eisenhower met with his staff and senior commanders again at 4:15 that very morning, Sunday, June 4, to reassess the situation. The 28-year-old Stagg, whom Eisenhower described as a "dour but canny Scot," confirmed his earlier, equally dour forecast: A high-pressure system was moving out, a low coming in. The weather on June 5, the Scotsman reported, was to be overcast and stormy, with a cloud base of 500 to 0 feet and Force-5 winds (19 to 24 miles per hour).

The success or failure of the invasion hinged on the weather. A calm sea was needed for the invasion fleet, low tides for the landing craft, and a bright moon for the paratroopers who would jump into Normandy the night before the beach landings. Only a few days in June met all of these requirements.

Even as Stagg spoke, numerous elements of the invasion fleet were embarking from British ports and making for "Picadilly Circus"—nickname of the fleet rendezvous area in the English Channel, centered 15 miles southeast of the Isle of Wight. Several thousand additional ships and vessels of every size and shape imaginable, carrying 170,000 troops, were in port or at anchor awaiting orders to sail. A mighty air armada of 10,521 aircraft stood waiting on British airfields.

Thousands of ships and aircraft, as well as 170,000 troops, waited at the ready for Dwight Eisenhower to give the command for the start of the D Day invasion. As stormy weather threatened the success of the operation, the Supreme Allied Commander faced a difficult decision—should he risk the lives of so many soldiers when their success was tentative, or should he wait for over a month for the possibility of better conditions?

Admiral Sir Bertram Ramsey cautioned Eisenhower that poor visibility and high seas would badly reduce the accuracy of supporting naval gunfire and that rough water would render the small landing craft hard to control. And

Air Chief Marshal Sir Trafford Leigh-Mallory warned that his bombers could not operate in the heavy cloud cover that Stagg predicted. With impaired naval operations and without air supremacy, the Allied invasion plan became too risky. Eisenhower had little choice but to postpone D Day—the start of the Normandy invasion—until June 6.

On June 4, however, the weather had steadily deteriorated during the day and now jeopardized the June 6 start date. A second postponement might delay the invasion for another two weeks, until the moon and tides cycled again in favor of the landings. Of course, there wasn't any certainty of good weather in two weeks. For the second time in two days, Eisenhower found himself facing the greatest and gravest decision that any commander in World War II would be called upon to make. This time, however, Captain Stagg offered a more optimistic forecast to the beleaguered commander.

"I think we have found a gleam of hope for you, sir," Stagg said. "The mass of weather fronts coming in from the Atlantic is moving faster than we anticipated." Stagg went on to predict "rather fair conditions" starting on the afternoon of Monday, June 5, and lasting until late in the evening of Tuesday, June 6. Stagg's extended forecast indicated more unsettled weather beyond Tuesday night. His prediction added up to a 36-hour window of favorable weather—an opening just big enough for the initial assault force to slip through. But should Eisenhower risk all—the lives of thousands of Allied troops and support personnel, the success of the invasion, and even the outcome of the war—on the strength of a weather report that might change many times before "H hour," the hour scheduled for the start of the operation on D Day?

On the other hand, any further delay might play havoc with the Allied timetable. Eisenhower no doubt considered how a lost month in starting the invasion of Russia in 1941 had cost Adolf Hitler, Chancellor of Germany, dearly when the onset of winter stopped his armies at the gates of Moscow. A 30-day delay in landing the Allied armies at Normandy might mean spending the winter on Germany's fortified western border—the "West Wall"—rather than pushing through it in the autumn.

While gusting winds and a driving rain rattled the windowpanes in the mess room's French doors, Eisenhower polled his chief subordinates with mixed results. Some said go. Others said no. Admiral Ramsey underscored the need for making a decision right away. "If Overlord [the Allied code name for the invasion of Normandy] is to proceed on Tuesday [June 6] I must issue provisional warning to my forces within the next half-hour." The air marshals, Sir Trafford Leigh-Mallory and Sir Arthur Tedder, expressed skepticism as to the effectiveness of air support under what Stagg had characterized as likely scattered-cloud conditions. Tedder said that a decision to go would be "chancy" and wanted another postponement.

Eisenhower then jutted his chin toward Major General Walter B. Smith, his chief of staff, and demanded, "What do you think?"

"It's a helluva gamble but it's the best possible gamble," Smith replied.

Eisenhower next turned abruptly to ground troop commander General Sir Bernard L. Montgomery and asked, "Do you see any reason why we should not go on Tuesday?"

Montgomery responded immediately with resounding emphasis. "No," he said, "I would say—Go!"

Eisenhower began to pace, head lowered, chin tucked against his chest, hands clasped behind his back. Smith watched his superior pacing and sensed the "loneliness and isolation of a commander at a time when such a momentous decision was to be taken by him, with full knowledge that failure or success rests on his individual decision."

Ike stopped pacing for a moment and asked of no one in particular, "The question is just how long can you hang this operation on the end of a limb and let it hang there?" No one answered and Ike resumed pacing. At 9:45 P.M., he stopped again and declared, "I don't see how we can possibly do anything else." Pending a final confirmation of Stagg's latest forecast the next morning, the invasion was on.

At 4:15 A.M. on Monday, June 5, Eisenhower convened another meeting. Stagg again brought good news. He predicted that the fair weather interval would likely extend well into Tuesday afternoon. Eisenhower grinned and said, "OK. Let's go."

Meanwhile, across the English Channel on the German-held side of the narrow waterway, anxious defenders continued their watch for the long-awaited Allied invasion. As they girded for the inevitable assault, talk about the weather dominated their conversations. The Germans knew that the invasion—when it came—would not commence until weather conditions favored such a massive operation. From top-level commanders to rank-and-file soldiers, German coastal defenders along the shore kept two eyes seaward and one ear out for the latest weather forecast. And each day, from Calais to Cherbourg, they asked one question more than any other: "Are they coming?"

On June 5, at German Seventh Army headquarters in Le Mans, Colonel General Friedrich Dollman asked his chief of staff, "Anything likely to happen today?"

Field Marshall Erwin Rommel visits a heavy artillery battery, part of the Atlantic Wall of German defenses. Rommel was also known as the Desert Fox for victories in Africa, and was named by Hitler as the Commander of German Army Group B and military overlord of the entire French coast.

Major General Max Pemsel, who had already checked with meteorologists in Paris, reported that foul weather predictions would seem to make an enemy landing unlikely. But Pemsel added doubtfully, "If only one could rely on those weather men."

That evening, on the east coast of the Cotentin Peninsula, 75 miles from the mouth of the Seine, a platoon of 3rd Company, 919th Infantry Regiment, was holding strongpoint No. 5. Second Lieutenant Arthur Jahnke was making an inspection round, threading his way along the most seaward trench line on the crest of a sand dune. Jahnke found a lookout peering through a mounted telescope. "Anything?" he asked.

"No news, Herr Leutnant," the lookout replied.

Jahnke stepped up to the telescope and looked for himself, across the nearshore and out toward the sea. The night was black. Rain clouds shrouded a full moon that broke through the clouds only occasionally and shone its pale light on the beach below. Farther inland, it briefly illuminated the hedgerows, willow trees, and flooded orchards of Normandy. Then, it would hide behind another scudding cloud mass, and the night would turn black again, as though someone had flipped an off switch.

"They won't come in this weather," the lookout volunteered. Jahnke concurred.

Rear Admiral Walter Hennecke, the German naval commander at Normandy, spent that same evening entertaining guests at a party held in his headquarters in Cherbourg. Earlier in the day he had requested a weather report from the chief of his meteorological station at Cap de la Hague and had received a reassuring response: "Rough sea, poor visibility, Force 5–6 [19–31 miles per hour] wind, rain likely to get heavier. Most probably we shan't even get our usual air raids." A comforting report, but the admiral wanted more.

"And what's it going to be like to-morrow?" he asked.

"There is little prospect of short-term changes in the weather during the next few days," the weather chief answered.

Hennecke beamed visibly. Thinking out loud, he said, "That means that the various conditions of tide, moon, and general weather situation necessary for a landing here in Northern France won't coincide again until the second half of June." The admiral no doubt felt relieved at what he likely felt was at least a two-week respite from the threat of imminent invasion. In reality, his sense of well-being would last but a few more hours. Nor was Hennecke the only high-ranking German commander to be lulled into a false sense of security by the bad weather and reports of more of the same.

On the morning of June 5, Field Marshal Erwin Rommel, commander of Army Group B and military overlord of the entire northern French coast, felt secure enough to leave his headquarters in France and drive to Herrlingen, Germany. He planned to celebrate his wife's birthday on June 6, then drive on to Berchtesgaden, Adolf Hitler's Bavarian retreat, for a conference with Germany's Führer (leader). Rommel hoped to persuade Hitler to transfer two additional armored divisions and another mortar brigade to Normandy. "The most urgent problem is to win the Führer over by personal conversation," Rommel wrote in his diary. At the time, Rommel did not realize just how urgent the problem was—but he was about to find out.

■   ■   ■

While Admiral Hennecke partied in Cherbourg and Field Marshal Rommel motored into Germany, the greatest invasion fleet ever assembled had been rendezvousing in the middle of the English Channel from British ports stretching from Wales to the North Sea. As midnight of

Eisenhower speaks with paratroopers, the all-important first soldiers to begin the invasion of Normandy, before they board their transports to France. Many parachuted wide of their intended target, drowned, or were shot by German soldiers. The paratroopers still captured several important military targets and key features of the terrain.

June 5 drew near, the Allied armada began bearing down on the coast of Normandy.

▦   ▦   ▦

Forty minutes after midnight, Lieutenant Colonel Hoffman stepped out of his bunker at the German battle headquarters of the 3rd Battalion, 919th Grenadier

Regiment, near Montebourg, and peered skyward. He sighted a flurry of white, mushroom-like blossoms, clearly visible in the then-moonlit sky. Momentarily stunned, he watched them float silently to earth before the reality of the moment overcame his shock: he was witnessing an airborne parachute attack. "Alarm! Enemy parachutists!" he shouted. "Alarm! Alarm!" The men of his battalion sprang into action.

German carbines began barking at the airborne enemy. Hoffman seized a rifle and opened fire on the descending parachutes. Dark clouds masked the moon and turned the sky black. Then, the first burst of fire from an American submachine gun clattered in the darkness. The long wait had finally ended. And Operation NEPTUNE—the attack phase of OVERLORD and the climactic battle of World War II in Europe—had begun.

It was June 6, 1944.

Operation OVERLORD: Planning and Preparing

Russian Marshal Joseph Stalin, U.S. President Franklin Delano Roosevelt, and British Prime Minster Winston Churchill, or the "Big Three," were the leaders of the Allied Powers against Germany, Italy, and Japan, known as the Axis Powers. The Big Three met face-to-face for the first time in Tehran, Iran, in December 1943 to coordinate war efforts and discuss postwar goals.

"The best that we could hope for was to deceive [the Germans] as to where and when the assault would come, so that they would prepare to meet us in the wrong place."

—Lieutenant General Omar N. Bradley,
U.S. 1st Army commander on D Day, June 6, 1944
(in Omar N. Bradley and Clair Blair, *A General's Life*)

After Germany's humiliating defeat in World War I by the Allied Powers—mainly Great Britain, France, Russia, Italy, and, beginning in 1917, the United States—Adolf Hitler rose to power as chancellor and dictator of Germany in 1933. Playing on political and economic unrest in post–World War I Germany, and promising to restore Germany to a position of European (if not world) dominance, Hitler embarked at once on an expansionist agenda.

Under the Nazi banner (Nazi was short for *National-sozialist,* the National Socialist German Workers' Party), Hitler initiated a program of nationalism, rearmament, political aggression, and racism, particularly anti-Semitism. On September 1, 1939, Hitler sent his armies crashing into Poland in pursuit of more *Lebensraum* (living space) for the German people. Two days later, Great Britain and France declared war on Germany, and World War II—the largest, most devastating war in history—began.

In the spring of 1940, the armies of Hitler's *blitzkrieg* (lightning war) smashed across western Europe, driving the British and French armies into a forced evacuation at Dunkirk. France surrendered to Germany three weeks later. And England stood alone.

■　　　■　　　■

Shortly after the humbling evacuation of Allied troops at Dunkirk (from May 26 to June 3, 1940) and the subsequent fall of France (June 22), Allied leaders began looking forward to the day when they could return to the European continent and reverse the fortunes of war against the Germans. In October 1941, British prime minister Winston Churchill appointed Lord Louis Mountbatten as the new head of Combined Operations and charged him with investigating the feasibility of amphibious operations in Europe.

"You are to prepare for the invasion of Europe," Churchill directed Mountbatten, "for unless we can go and land and fight Hitler and beat his forces on land, we shall never win this war. You must devise and

Adolf Hitler became chancellor and dictator of Germany in 1933, promising to seek revenge for "humiliations" suffered in World War I. His politics also demanded the superiority of white, heterosexual Christian Germans above all other nationalities and minorities. Hitler ultimately controlled all defense decisions and troop movements during the war from his safe refuge far away in Germany.

design the appliances, the landing craft and the technique to enable us to effect a landing against opposition and to maintain ourselves there." And if that were not task enough, Churchill added, "The whole of the south coast of England is a bastion of defence against the invasion of Hitler: you've got to turn it into the springboard for attack."

Mountbatten set about his formidable assignment at once. He prepared for raids along the entire enemy coastline from North Cape to the Bay of Biscay, lending special emphasis to a return to France. To make the invasion possible, Mountbatten was to develop apparatus and equipment, select and build up bases from which an assault could be launched, establish amphibious training centers, and target the landing site for attack.

Although critics would later charge Churchill with favoring a return to Europe by way of its "soft underbelly" along the Mediterranean, Mountbatten never doubted the prime minister's intention. "It was Winston who first saw the need for the cross-Channel business, and who wanted it on the proper scale," Mountbatten said later. "I was to have 200,000 men trained a year hence, and another 100,000 six months later."

Hitler upped the stakes in the war by invading the Soviet Union on June 22, 1941, in pursuit of more *Lebensraum*. Britain now had an ally of sorts in the Soviets. But Churchill still cherished his long-held idea that the United States would eventually join the war on Britain's side and guarantee the defeat of Germany and its allies, known collectively as the Axis powers, or simply the Axis. (Germany, Italy, and Japan comprised the principal member nations of the Axis by virtue of the Tripartite Pact, signed on September 27, 1940. The pact called for each to lend military assistance in case of attack by any nation not yet in the war, a statement clearly aimed at the United States.)

The Americans opposed Japan's aggressive expansion in Asia, and the Japanese felt challenged by the United States for dominance in the Far East and Pacific. Thus,

Montbatten was directed by the British prime minister in 1941 to begin planning a counterattack on Germany. U.S. and Russian forces were welcomed as allies and invited to join the planning after Germany invaded the Soviet Union and Japan bombed the American naval base in Hawaii. The U.S.-planned Operation BOLERO included Operation SLEDGEHAMMER, but was replaced by British Operation TORCH, the precursor to Operation OVERLORD, the initial phase of which was Operation NEPTUNE (D Day on June 6, 1944).

after the Japanese attacked the U.S. naval base at Pearl Harbor on December 7, 1941—a date that President Franklin D. Roosevelt proclaimed would "live in infamy"— the U.S. Congress declared war on Japan the next day. Germany and Italy declared war on the United States three days later.

Churchill welcomed his American allies with a sense of relief and elation. "No American will think it wrong of me if I proclaim that to have the United States at our side was to me the greatest joy," he wrote after the war. "I could not foretell the course of events. . . . [B]ut now at this very moment I knew the United States was in the war, up to the neck and in to the death." To Churchill—after Dunkirk, the fall of France, the Battle of Britain, and innumerable other wartime setbacks—America's entry into the war meant that "we had won after all." At the same time, it made Mountbatten's already difficult task a little tougher and a lot more complex.

As early as November 1940, the U.S. Joint Board—predecessor of the U.S. Joint Chiefs of Staff—had agreed that if the United States found itself at war with both Germany and Japan, priority must be given to defeating Germany. This meant waging a defensive war in the Pacific while vigorously prosecuting the war in the European theater, where the major threat lay.

At the first Washington conference (code-named ARCADIA) from December 22, 1941, to January 14, 1942, at which Churchill and Roosevelt and their military advisers hammered out war plans and future strategy, representatives of both governments saw no reason to change the Joint Board's earlier decision to defeat Germany first. They also agreed to merge the British and U.S. Joint Chiefs of Staff (JCS) into the Combined Chiefs of Staff (CCS) to oversee and direct strategic operations. With the Russians locked in a battle for survival with the Germans on the eastern front, the key questions that now faced the two western Allies became when and where they would start a second front. It would take them nearly two more years of quarreling to agree on the answers.

During the first months of 1942, both sides prepared their positions for further negotiations. In March 1942, U.S. Army chief of staff General George C. Marshall submitted a memorandum to President Roosevelt containing a proposed course of future action under the overall code name of BOLERO. General Marshall's chief planner was a previously little known brigadier general named Dwight D. Eisenhower. Under his direction, the War Plans Division had drafted the BOLERO plan contained in what soon became known as the Marshall Memorandum.

BOLERO called for an immediate buildup of U.S. forces and matériel in Britain, aimed at launching a cross-Channel invasion in 1943 (tentatively code-named ROUND-UP). Marshall believed that the United States should strike back against Germany as soon as possible, reasoning that a democracy would not long support indecision and inaction. Marshall's proposal also included a contingency plan (called SLEDGEHAMMER) that provided for a limited invasion of the European continent in 1942 in the event of either a German internal collapse or an imminent Soviet military collapse.

On April 1, Roosevelt accepted the BOLERO plan and sent Harry L. Hopkins, his personal assistant, and Marshall to London to solicit British approval. Despite misgivings over SLEDGEHAMMER contingencies that might force even a limited cross-Channel foray as early as the fall of 1942, the British approved the American plan "in principle." As the Americans were to find out shortly, many a discord can arise twixt principle and performance.

In Washington, Dwight Eisenhower—who had grown distressed over the possible dispersion of troops, ships, and supplies to meet immediate crises arising in the Pacific, Africa, the Middle East, and the Far East—felt elated over the British acceptance of the plan. He noted: "[A]t long last, and after months of struggle . . . we are all definitely committed to one concept of fighting! If we can agree on major purposes and objectives, our efforts will begin to fall in line and we won't just be thrashing around in the dark."

To Eisenhower and the American war planners, BOLERO offered a number of attractive features and the soundest strategy for offensive operations in Europe. It provided for an all-out bombing campaign against Germany's vitals, culminating in an assault on the northwest coast of France using the British Isles as a staging (assembly) area and springboard. Logistically, the plan represented the shortest route from the United States to the heart of Germany. Operating from a ready-made base in Britain precluded the need for carrier-based air cover to support ground troops and enabled the development of air superiority over the enemy in northern France.

Additionally, BOLERO would furnish a long-term strategic goal for industrial and personnel mobilization, satisfy Marshall's insistence on early decisive action (1943), and fulfill the military dictum of concentration of forces. (The dictum stresses keeping forces together to achieve and maintain numerical superiority, allowing detachments only under the most urgent situations.) The plan would also satisfy the increasing demands of Soviet leader Joseph Stalin for a second front.

Plans to move ahead with BOLERO began at once. Eisenhower arrived in Britain to assume command in the European theater on June 24, 1942, and American forces and matériel began pouring into the British Isles. But British reluctance soon surfaced regarding the prospect of a second front in Europe as early as 1943. The Americans quickly discovered that the British acceptance of BOLERO "in principle" really meant something like "we've got a better idea."

A few days earlier, Churchill had flown by Boeing Clipper to confer again with Roosevelt, first in the president's Hyde Park retreat in New York and then at the White House in Washington. Churchill feared that Roosevelt, with his growing demands for action in 1942, "was getting a little off the rails." Even more, he feared that an attempt to mount a cross-Channel attack before stronger forces could be amassed might end in an Allied bloodbath. Instead, Churchill hoped to persuade Roosevelt that a better immediate course of action might lie in an American landing in Morocco and Algeria.

The prime minister's alternative—code-named TORCH—would enable the Allies to squeeze Field Marshal Erwin Rommel's Afrika Korps and its allied Italian forces between the Americans in the west and British in the east, and ultimately to drive all Axis forces from the African continent. North Africa would then provide an ideal platform from which to attack Europe's so-called soft underbelly.

In July 1942, Roosevelt sent Hopkins, Marshall, and Admiral Ernest J. King, navy commander in chief, to London for further talks. These discussions yielded the decision to invade French North Africa in the autumn of 1942. As a result, TORCH then replaced BOLERO. Anglo-American agreement over BOLERO had lasted less than three months.

Allied leaders delayed plans to invade France in 1943 and eventually postponed them until 1944. Consequently, the Combined Chiefs of Staff called on Eisenhower, now elevated to the rank of lieutenant general, to put aside his responsibilities in Britain to direct the North African landings.

At the start of 1943, while American and British troops were battling Rommel's Axis forces in North Africa, Churchill and Roosevelt and their chiefs of staff met again, this time at Anfa, a suburb of Casablanca, in French Morocco (January 14 to 24). Stalin had also been invited to attend the conference (code-named SYMBOL) but declined because of the critical fighting at Stalingrad. They discussed future strategy and agreed on several key objectives. They conceded that the invasion of France would probably need to be postponed until 1944. In the interim, the two leaders agreed to accelerate the war against German U-boats (submarines) in the Atlantic; to launch a combined bomber offensive from Britain against Germany; to move Allied forces into Sicily and Italy after clearing North Africa; and to seek the "unconditional surrender" of Germany, Italy, and Japan.

In March 1943, so that plans and preparations for the invasion of the Continent in 1944 could proceed, the Combined Chiefs appointed Lieutenant General Sir Frederick E. Morgan as Chief of Staff to the Supreme Allied Commander (COSSAC) designate. (Lord Mountbatten continued to serve as a member of the Chiefs of Staff until he was appointed Supreme Commander of the Southeast Asia Command as a full admiral in August 1943.) Morgan's many duties included establishing a headquarters for the yet-unnamed supreme commander and drafting an outline plan for the Normandy landing. Morgan and a small staff started work on the plan (Operation ROUNDHAMMER, later called OVER-LORD) at once, based on a target date of May 1, 1944, and an operating strength of 29 divisions built up in Britain.

At the first Quebec conference (code-named QUADRANT) from August 17 to 24, 1943, Churchill, Roosevelt, and the Combined Chiefs endorsed Morgan's

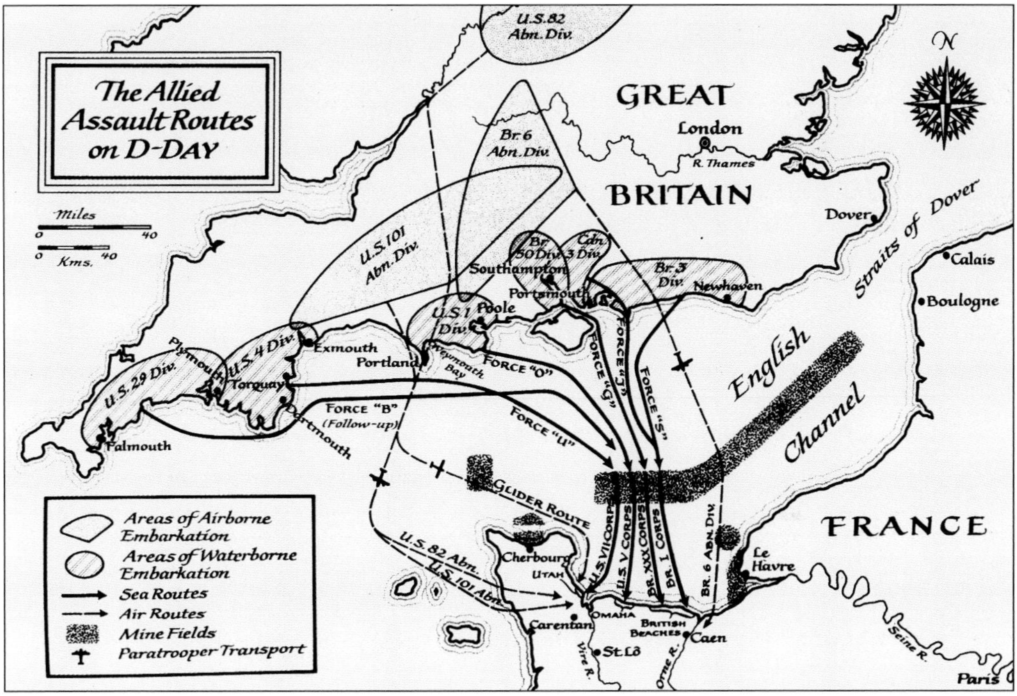
The Allied Assault Routes on D-DAY
GREAT
BRITAIN
London
R. Thames
Dover
Straits of Dover
Calais
Boulogne
English
Channel
FRANCE
Le Havre
Caen
Paris
Seine R.
U.S.82 Abn. Div.
Br. 6 Abn. Div.
U.S.101 Abn. Div.
Br. 50 Div.
Cdn. 3 Div.
Br. 3 Div.
Southampton
Portsmouth
Newhaven
U.S.1 Div.
Poole
Exmouth
Portland
Weymouth Bay
U.S.4 Div.
Torquay
Plymouth
U.S.29 Div.
Dartmouth
Falmouth
FORCE "O"
FORCE "B" (Follow-up)
FORCE "U"
FORCE "G"
FORCE "J"
FORCE "S"
GLIDER ROUTE
U.S.82 Abn.
U.S.101 Abn.
Cherbourg
UTAH
OMAHA
BRITISH BEACHES
Carentan
St.Lô
Vire R.
Orne R.
U.S.VII CORPS
U.S.V CORPS
BR.XXX CORPS
BR.I CORPS
BR.6 ABN. DIV.
Miles
0
40
Kms.
Areas of Airborne Embarkation
Areas of Waterborne Embarkation
Sea Routes
Air Routes
Mine Fields
Paratrooper Transport

The whole south of England turned into a supply depot to provide manpower, transportation, supplies, and weaponry to support the huge invasion. Several new landing craft, artificial harbors, other engineering feats, and innovative war strategies were used very successfully in Normandy.

Normandy plan and gave the go-ahead for the construction of artificial harbors called Mulberries. The detailed planning was then passed on to the responsible air, land, and sea commanders involved in the operation. Morgan took on increased power and responsibilities and became the driving force behind OVERLORD and the myriad tasks associated with it.

These tasks, to name only a few, included such diverse elements as intelligence, subversive warfare, deception, meteorological intelligence, the preparation of the Mulberries, the laying of cross-Channel fuel lines called PLUTOs (an acronym for Pipe Line Under The

Ocean) to supply fuel for the invasion forces, and civil affairs. The latter triggered so many heated discussions between London and Washington that Morgan felt compelled to remark that "there were plenty of affairs but the difficulty was to keep them civil."

Two Mulberries were built at sites around Britain—one for British use at Arromanches, the other for American use at St. Laurent. The parts for the two artificial harbors comprised some 400 units weighing about 1.5 million tons. When completed, the two behemoths were towed to Britain's south coast and submerged to avoid detection by the Germans. (After D Day, they were raised and towed across the Channel in an operation involving 132 tugs and 10,000 men. Kenneth Bungard, one of those men, later remarked: "When I got back to my girlfriend, I told her I'd spent my war sailing round the ocean on an office block—which is the only way I could describe it, really!")

In 1942, a trial PLUTO—a flexible pipe—had been laid by Combined Operations across the Bristol Channel, after which preparations were made to lay four more from the Isle of Wight to Cherbourg. These were projected to pump up to one million gallons of oil and fuel. (In January 1945, 16 more pipes were laid from Dungeness to Ambleteuse, delivering up to 4,000 gallons a day.)

Along with the foregoing engineering marvels, "Hobart's Funnies"—specially modified tanks and armored vehicles for clearing beaches under fire—were destined to play a crucial role on British and Canadian beaches on D Day. Under the direction of Major General Sir Percy Hobart, commander of the British 79th Armored Division and a pioneer of tank warfare, subordinates developed several "funny" vehicles: "flail" tanks for clearing lanes through mine fields by "flailing" the ground in front of them with weighted chains extended on rotating drums that detonated explosives in their path; tank "dozers" fitted with bulldozer blades for filling in ditches and road craters and clearing other obstacles under fire; "arks," turretless tanks with front and rear ramps that would drive into obstacles, lower their ramps, and form bridges for other tanks to drive over; and a number of others, including multipurpose AVREs (Armored Vehicles Royal Engineers) designed to carry a variety of devices for crossing ditches, breaching concrete obstacles, and clearing rubble.

One especially fearsome Funny was a modified Churchill Mark 7 tank called the "Crocodile," a flame-throwing tank designed to incinerate any obstacle within a 360-foot range. Lieutenant Kenneth Macksey, of the 141st Regiment, Royal Armored Corps, later recalled: "I don't think that anybody wanted to flame Germans in particular. It was rather a repugnant job, but it had to be done."

While preparations for the landing in France pro-gressed in Britain, British and American troops completed the ouster of German and Italian forces from North Africa in May 1943. The Allied victory in North Africa opened the door for subsequent invasions in the Mediterranean— Sicily in July 1943 and the Italian mainland in September 1943—under the overall command of Dwight Eisenhower. As 1943 drew to a close, the Allied leaders met again, this time at the Tehran Conference (code-named EUREKA), and this time with Soviet leader Joseph Stalin joining Churchill and Roosevelt.

The "Big Three," as they were called, finally reached agreement on the necessity for establishing a second front in northwest France. (British leaders had proposed an alternative front in the Balkans or a stepped-up effort in Italy, but Stalin had pressed hard for northern

France.) At the end of their meeting, the three leaders initialed a document that summarized, wrote Churchill, "the military conclusions of our Triple Conference" in five short paragraphs. The fourth paragraph noted that "Operation 'Overlord' would be launched during May 1944." It also "took note of Marshal Stalin's statement that the Soviet forces would launch an offensive at about the same time with the object of preventing the German forces from transferring from the Eastern to the Western Front."

The die was cast, the commitment made. There would be no turning back.

Events moved quickly now. The Combined Chiefs appointed General Eisenhower as Supreme Allied Commander on Christmas Eve, 1943. Eisenhower returned to London in January 1944 to set up his headquarters (SHAEF) and select his principal subordinates. The supreme commander announced his choices on February 14, 1944: British air chief marshal Sir Arthur W. Tedder, deputy supreme commander; British general Sir Bernard L. Montgomery, commander in chief of ground forces; U.S. lieutenant general Omar N. Bradley, commander of U.S. ground forces; British admiral Bertram H. Ramsey, chief of the combined naval forces; and British air chief marshal Sir Trafford Leigh-Mallory, commander of the combined air forces. Eisenhower and his SHAEF staff now assumed full responsibility for finalizing the plans and preparations for Operation OVERLORD.

The final invasion plans developed by SHAEF planners called for the British 2nd Army to land on beaches designated Gold, Juno, and Sword, north of Caen and Bayeux. The U.S. 1st Army was to move ashore west of the British on beaches designated Utah, due east of Ste. Mère-Église, and Omaha, north of the village of

A mock invasion force was gathered at Dover, England, near Calais, France under the control of General Patton to serve as decoy for the real invasion further south. Patton (left) is photographed here with Bradley, the commander of U.S. ground forces, and Montgomery, commander in chief of ground forces. Many branches of various military services from many nations worked together to defeat the German forces in June 1944.

Trévères. The landings were set to commence at dawn. They were to be preceded by airborne drops several hours earlier at either end of the assault zone, so that para-troopers could seize control of critical bridgeheads and roadways to prevent the flow of enemy reinforcements.

The objectives of OVERLORD were several and the Allied forces, once ashore, were expected to achieve them within three months. Their first goal was to drive inland and secure a sizeable beachhead in western France between the Seine and Loire Rivers. This lodgment, once established, would provide the Allies with ports to sustain and build up their forces, airfields from which to fly ground-support missions, maneuvering room to maximize the effectiveness of their mechanized forces, and sites for locating headquarters, replacement and supply depots, and all other installations and facilities essential to modern armies. At this point, Eisenhower planned to pause and regroup his forces, then break through the enemy's containing forces, attack toward the German border, and ultimately smash across the Rhine River and into the Ruhr Valley, the heart of German industry.

To implement this master plan, U.S. troops and supplies poured into Britain at a phenomenal rate during the first few months of 1944. The flow of troops and matériel turned the south of England into a bristling armed camp with some 1,627,000 American soldiers and 53,000 sailors, accompanied by a huge armada of warships, supply ships, and landing craft. General Eisenhower called this vast assemblage "a great human spring, coiled for the moment when its energy should be released and it would vault the English Channel in the greatest amphibious assault ever assembled."

The Allies could not hope to keep the buildup a secret from German intelligence, so they initiated a massive disinformation campaign under the code name FORTITUDE. The SHAEF planners created an entirely fictitious army—the First U.S. Army Group, or FUSAG—under the supposed command of Lieutenant General George S. Patton, well known to the Germans as an aggressive leader in North Africa and Sicily. (Actually, Patton had arrived in

This watercolor painting by U.S. Navy Combat Artist Dwight C. Shepler shows U.S. soldiers practicing a large scale invasion, using flamethrowers, amphibious vehicles, landing craft, and huge amounts of munitions. Would circumstances and terrain in Normandy be similar enough to the rolling hills of Devon, England, to prove this practice valuable?

England to take charge of the U.S. 3rd Army, slated to spearhead the projected Allied breakout in Normandy.)

Under Patton's direction, the Allies built an intricate bogus headquarters at Dover, across from Calais. Additionally, Patton's people filled the Dover area with sham vehicles and equipment, troop encampments populated with soldiers not scheduled to take part in the initial phase of OVERLORD (code-named NEPTUNE), and

Military intelligence and counterintelligence was used to great effect in the fake buildup of forces and munitions in Dover. News of the ruse was 35 to note key features such as the entrance to the harbor, patrol ship, and barrage balloon.

phony communications systems. They hoped to focus German attention there and deceive the enemy into thinking that the Normandy landing, when it occurred, was only a feint and that the main invasion forces would actually land at Calais.

Simultaneous with the fake buildup in Dover and the real buildup in the south of England, British intelligence agencies leaked misinformation about the "Calais Invasion" to known German agents. British official history records would later characterize this monumental sham as "the most complex and successful deception operation in the entire history of war."

In the last months before the scheduled landing, Allied aircraft waged an intensive bombing campaign, demolishing vital bridges, railheads, and other military and industrial targets in Belgium and France, and carrying out a rash of diversionary strikes in the Calais area. In the meantime, the Allied "spring" of men, ships, and supplies coiled ever tighter.

SHAEF planners left no task undone that might contribute to an Allied victory in this historically massive and unique undertaking. The Allies stockpiled tanks, vehicles, arms and ammunition, rations, barbed wire, and medical supplies. Beyond the ordinary paraphernalia of modern warfare, they collected and staged bulldozers, fleets of buses, railway locomotives, power plants, entire field hospitals, radio stations, police stations, prison cages, bakeries, laundries, and telephone exchanges, to say nothing of staggering reserves of food, clothing, and fuel, along with a prodigious supply of French money. Perhaps historian Robert Leckie said it best when he suggested that, once under way, the invasion force would constitute "nothing less than a large modern city sailing to battle."

Such was the colossus gathered in the south of England on June 5, 1944, awaiting orders from the supreme commander of Operation OVERLORD to "spring" into action. The orders came barely a moment after General Eisenhower reached his historic decision. A terse message was flashed to the fleet: "PROCEED WITH OPERATION NEPTUNE."

The Atlantic Wall:
German Defenders
and Defenses

German tanks, called panzers, were the largest moveable artillery available. Hitler weakened the defense of the French coast by moving troops and panzers to fight Russians on the Eastern Front. Their loss was sorely felt since the German navy and Luftwaffe (air force) were virtually powerless to provide resistance during the upcoming invasion.

> *"The coastline of Europe will, in the coming months, be exposed to the danger of an enemy landing in force."*
>
> —Adolf Hitler, in Directive No. 40, March 23, 1942

The Germans knew that the Allies were coming, of course, and had been preparing their defenses for many months. But the Germans did not know precisely *when* or *where* the Allies would choose to strike. Accordingly, on December 14, 1941, Hitler issued orders for the defense of the Atlantic coastline. His strategic objective was "to assure protection against any landing operation

Adolf Hitler (right) plans German war strategy with members of his staff at headquarters. The rank and authority he gave Marshal von Rundstedt was greatly undermined by the liberty and discretion he gave Marshal Rommel. Similar contradictions in policy and defense movements hampered the attainment of German military objectives.

even of very considerable strength with the employment of the smallest possible number of static forces."

At that time, Hitler still considered Norway as the most likely target for an Allied invasion. Commando raids on the Norwegian coast during the week after Christmas 1941 supported his fears. Even so, his order of the 14th placed greater importance on the coasts of Belgium and France than previously. Lieutenant General Walter Warlimont, deputy chief of the operations staff of the OKW (*Oberkommando der Wehrmacht,* or High Command of the Armed Forces),

One of Rommel's additions to the coast fortification was the invention of these mined spikes set on the beaches at the low-water level. When the tide and an invading flotilla came in, the mines would explode against the boats' hulls and destroy them. The mined spikes were just one of the many obstacles encountered by Allied forces on D Day.

noted: "In the light of subsequent developments, and looked at over-all, this order, whether intentionally or not, marks the beginning of the period when, strategically, Germany was forced on to the defensive."

Construction began on a line of fortifications along the Atlantic coastline in early 1942. Hitler, who served as supreme commander of Germany's armed forces, called it

Comparing the Opponents

A brief comparison of the Allied and German armies reveals that the opposing forces at Normandy shared much in common. The basic infantry weapons on both sides were bolt-action or semiautomatic rifles. Their rates of fire and ranges exceeded the needs of most firefights, which usually occurred at distances of less than 300 yards. Although all soldiers on both sides received training as infantrymen, only a small minority ever fired a shot in anger at the enemy.

A squad or section formed the basic tactical unit and usually included about 10 such riflemen plus a light or medium machine gun capable of firing efficiently at a rate of 200 rounds a minute. Enumerating broadly, three squads formed a platoon, three platoons a company, and three companies a battalion. Military units from a company upward contained a headquarters component and received supplemental reinforcements of weaponry and equipment. The battalion represented the soldier's extended family and comprised about 800 men, plus a varying number and assortment of vehicles (as determined by its organizational specialty), about 12 guns for artillery, and some 50 tanks for armor.

Three battalions made up a regiment and three regiments formed a division, the smallest unit capable of operating independently in the field. A division fielded anywhere from 10,000 to 20,000 soldiers, depending on troop availability and reinforcements. A corps comprised three or more divisions, three or more corps made up an army, and two or more armies constituted an army group.

The principal tanks used at Normandy were the American M4 Sherman, the British Cromwell, and the German Panzer IV. All three were roughly equal in fighting qualities. Infantry antitank weapons included the American bazooka (named after a musical device invented by American comedian Bob Burns) and the German *Panzerfaust* (tank fist). Their rocket projectiles could penetrate a tank's armor but were ineffective at ranges greater than 100 yards.

Propeller-driven, single-seat fighter-bomber aircraft provided close air support. Typically, they flew at a maximum speed of 400 miles an hour and carried an ordnance load of less than 2,000 pounds. German air support was conspicuously light and not a factor in the fighting.

the Atlantic Wall and delegated its construction to the Todt Organization, a semi-military governmental unit established in 1938 for building military installations and special highways suitable for armored vehicles. Eventually the Atlantic Wall stretched from the Netherlands to Spain—though not continuously—for some 1,670 miles. Describing the Wall as "a belt of strongpoints and gigantic fortifications," the Führer boasted that its defense line was "impregnable against every enemy."

To oversee and direct the defense of the Atlantic coastline, Hitler recalled to duty the twice-retired General Field Marshal Karl R. Gerd von Rundstedt and appointed him *Oberbefehlshaber West,* or OB West (commander in chief, west) in March 1942. Already an old man of 67 and well deserving of his nickname *Der Alte Herr* ("the Old Gentleman"), Rundstedt represented the best of the old Prussian officer corps. He was unflappable, honest, and loyal, and he often demonstrated a wry sense of humor. As a top-level commander, he exhibited thoroughness and flexibility, coupled with tactical and strategic skill. The dignified, aristocratic Rundstedt again answered the call of duty and established his headquarters at St. Germain, about 11 miles northwest of Paris on the Seine River.

Rundstedt faced a formidable task. His staff in OB West spent 1942 and 1943 attempting to forecast where the Allies might launch their attack. Potential invasion zones seemed limitless, with real possibilities stretching from Norway along the European coast to Spain and along the Mediterranean to Greece. In a postwar report prepared for the U.S. Army, General Günther von Blumentritt, Rundstedt's chief of staff, wrote: "Any layman knows that 'Fortress Europe' [a phrase used in German propaganda to denote Germany's supposedly impenetrable shield of defenses] could not be defended in a military sense by one people and one already weakened Wehrmacht [German armed forces]. . . . The Allies would have been successful at any point they chose to attack."

In 1942 and beyond, despite Blumentritt's pessimistic latter-day assessment of Germany's ability to defend the European continent, Hitler placed unwavering confidence in the deterrent capability of the Atlantic Wall. After several British commando raids in 1942, particularly the August 19 raid on Dieppe, the Führer ordered construction of the Wall to be pushed "fanatically." His new, accelerated schedule called for the completion of some 15,000 strong-points at principal ports and beaches by May 1, 1943. These strongpoints—fortified, steel-reinforced concrete structures impervious to bombing and naval bombardment—were to be manned by some 300,000 troops. Hitler's order was hopelessly unattainable in the time allotted.

Furthermore, OB West commander Gerd von Rundstedt did not share the Führer's infinite faith in the Atlantic Wall. "It had no depth and little surface," he explained later. "It was sheer humbug. . . . Once through the so-called Wall, the rest of these fortifications and fortresses facing the sea were of no use at all against an attack from behind. I reported all this to the Führer in October 1943, but it was not favorably received."

In that report, Rundstedt indicated that the coastal defenses were inadequate and that his forces were spread too thin. The old Prussian concluded that his command was only "conditionally ready for action." Hitler acted promptly to rectify the inadequacies reported by Rundstedt—inadequacies for which the Führer himself bore responsibility.

In May 1942, Hitler had instituted a policy that gave first priority for troops to be sent to the Russian front. Consequently, he was forced to garrison the west with only those troops whose wounds or other disabilities rendered them unfit to endure the severities of duty in the east.

General Field Marshal von Rundstedt, appointed commander in chief west, had decades of military experience by 1942. His almost-impossible task of predicting and preparing for an Allied invasion was made more difficult by Hitler's contradictory decisions and bad policies with which Runstedt frequently disagreed.

During the next year, 22 infantry and six armored divisions left France for the eastern front, taking with them the best men and equipment of the divisions left behind. Western replacements consisted primarily of overage soldiers or troops convalescing from wounds. Some units were made up of Italian, Polish, and Russian defectors. Although a few first-line units existed in the west, most had been scattered and shattered in the east. Moreover, western units were often armed with leftover weaponry of Czech or French manufacture, which created supply and maintenance problems. And the combat readiness of troops was frequently sacrificed when soldiers were used in crash efforts to build fortifications rather than to hone their fighting skills in training exercises.

On November 3, 1943, in an attempt to refocus German military priorities, Hitler issued his Directive No. 51, a basic order outlining the defense of the west. He noted that an enemy invasion of France would likely commence in the spring of 1944, probably in the Pas de Calais—the Strait of Dover. Hitler reprioritized his troop allocations. No more troops were to be withdrawn from the west without his personal approval. And western defenses were to be strengthened to the maximum extent possible, for "it is here—unless all indications are misleading—that the decisive battle against the landing forces will be fought." Hitler ended his directive in a troublesome way: "All persons in authority will guard against wasting time and energy in useless quibbling about jurisdictional matters and will direct all efforts toward strengthening our defensive and offensive power." If "quibbling" over command authority were to exist—as it would—Hitler had only himself to blame.

In theory, Hitler's chain of command in the west exemplified good order. Hitler, as supreme commander, stood at the top of the command hierarchy. At the next level down, the OKW (High Command), under Field Marshal Wilhelm Keitel, directed military activities (that is, carried out Hitler's orders) everywhere except in the Soviet Union. OB West, under the OKW, held responsibility for the coastal defense of Holland, Belgium, and France. Army

Groups B and G were directly subordinate to OB West.

Naval and air operations fell to Navy Group West and the Third Air Fleet, respectively, which, in turn, reported to the High Command of the Navy (*Oberkommando der Kriegsmarine,* or OKM) and the High Command of the Army (*Oberkommando der Heeres,* or OKH). These commands were subordinate to OB West only for the tactical defense of the coast, as were a number of local commands and Waffen-SS units (armed forces of Heinrich Himmler's *Schutzstaffel,* or SS, the elite guard of the Nazi Party).

Hitler intentionally spread authority across several commands so that no single element would become too powerful and thus pose a threat to his own authority. If command of the German forces in Normandy could be reduced to one person, that person was the Führer himself. He orchestrated German strategy from afar, poring over maps in the *Wolfsschanze*, or Wolf's Lair, as his field headquarters in East Prussia was called. His ability to respond rapidly to developing situations from a distance was to become problematical.

In the field, the convoluted chain of command was to prove cumbersome at best and disastrous at worst. Writing later of this confusing command structure, *panzer* (tank) group commander General Geyr von Schweppenburg observed, "It was impossible to obtain clear-cut decisions on the broader controversial issues. The ship was not steered; it drifted." And the already muddy water of command was about to become even murkier.

On November 6, only three days after issuing his Directive No. 51, the Führer, in typical Hitlerian fashion, complicated his chain of command still further. He designated Field Marshal Erwin Rommel as Commander Army Group for Special Employment with tactical command in the west in the event of an invasion. Hitler also assigned Rommel—the famed "Desert Fox" of the Afrika Korps—

the task of inspecting the western coastal defenses and drafting plans for defeating the anticipated Allied invasion. And on January 15, 1944, Hitler appointed Rommel commander of Army Group B under Rundstedt.

Although theoretically subordinate to Rundstedt, Rommel, at 51, now held an equal rank, exuded energy, and displayed a more forceful personality than his superior, who was now 69. Rommel's rank and charisma enabled him to exert far greater influence than his position would have normally allowed. Additionally, as a field marshal, he enjoyed the privilege of skirting the chain of command and communicating directly with the Führer. Rommel could thus undercut Rundstedt's authority whenever he wished—and he wished with considerable regularity.

Inevitably, the defense concepts of the younger man, the son of a schoolmaster and career officer who had associated himself with the Nazi Party to accelerate his advancement, would clash with the opinions of the aging Prussian aristocrat. Simply put, Rommel favored a defense on the beach only, whereas Rundstedt advocated a defense in depth. "The enemy is at his weakest just after landing," asserted Rommel. "The troops are unsure, and possibly even seasick. They are unfamiliar with the terrain. Heavy weapons are not yet available in sufficient quantity. That is the moment to strike at them and defeat them."

To this end, Rommel advocated a linear defensive structure close to the coastline, with heavy armaments, artillery, and tactical reserves deployed to the fullest extent and ready to engage the enemy on the beaches. He went over Rundstedt's head and applied personally to Hitler for command of five panzer divisions to be positioned no farther than four or five miles from the coast.

As defensive adjuncts, Rommel had the foreshore of beaches below the high-water mark lined with ramming cones of his own invention. The cones were affixed with mines and steel saws designed to wreck invading landing craft. On the beaches proper he ordered the dumping of hundreds of thousands of steel-girder obstacles and the implanting of millions of mines. "It is on the beaches that the fate of the invasion will be decided," Rommel insisted, "and, what is more, during the first twenty-four hours."

By contrast, Rundstedt and panzer commander General Geyr von Schweppenburg wanted to fight the decisive battle behind the coast. They placed greater reliance on armored forces and mechanized reserves, whose mobility and flexibility would enable them to respond quickly to an attacker's forward thrust. Their defense concept represented the tried-and-true strategic principle of encircling the enemy in order to defeat him. To implement his strategy, Rundstedt stationed a newly created armored command—Panzer Group West, under Schweppenburg—near Paris. He hoped to move the force, as events dictated, from Paris to the site of an enemy assault at either the Pas de Calais or Normandy.

Hitler initially agreed to Rommel's request for five panzer divisions but relented when Rundstedt objected strongly and returned control of the panzers to him. The Führer finally compromised in April 1944, having by then stationed 10 panzer divisions in the west. He consigned three panzer divisions to Rommel's Army Group B in Normandy, sent three others to General Johannes Blaskowitz's newly organized Army Group G south of the Loire River, and retained the remaining four divisions as the theater reserve under OKW control. Of the remaining 54 divisions now in France, Hitler allocated 35 divisions to Army Group B and 19 to Army Group G.

As a result of the Führer's compromise, Rundstedt became virtually superfluous except as a conduit between Hitler and the two army groups, which, theoretically, the old Prussian still commanded. A disgruntled Rundstedt

Rundstedt disagreed with Hitler's defense of the western European coast with the "Atlantic Wall." He believed the fortified installations and artillery points would be useless once the enemy was off the beach and moved more inland. Gun bunkers like this one were made of woven steel bars and then covered with concrete.

later said, "My sole prerogative was to change the guard at my gate." Furthermore, the redistribution of forces deprived both Rommel and Rundstedt of the decisive authority over armor that would become critical as the battle for France developed.

By the middle of May 1944, Rommel's Army Group B comprised General of Fliers Friedrich Christiansen's

(German) Armed Forces Netherlands (88th Corps), Colonel General Hans von Salmuth's Fifteenth Army, Colonel General Friedrich Dollman's Seventh Army—which would bear the brunt of the Allied invasion—plus two corps and three panzer divisions in reserve. (Neither Christiansen's corps nor Salmuth's Fifteenth Army would see action on D Day, the latter falling for the Allied ruse and being held in place at the Pas de Calais by General Patton's phantom First U.S. Army Group.)

Admiral Theodor Krancke's Navy Group West, operating with only five torpedo boats, 30 patrol boats, and 36 submarines, was assigned a purely defensive role in case of an invasion and would later offer little resistance against the massive Allied armada. And *Luftwaffe* (air force) field marshal Hugo Sperrle's Third Air Fleet represented an equally feeble defense force. On May 30, Sperrle could put only 497 aircraft aloft in the skies that would soon be darkened by thousands of Allied planes. Comparatively speaking, German naval and air presence at Normandy would border on the nonexistent.

As the days advanced into June, Rommel began to suspect that the invasion might come in the vicinity of the Bay of the Seine and the east coast of the Cotentin Peninsula. His growing suspicion caused him to shift a mobile division into the Cotentin area. He also wanted to send an armored division but Hitler refused, insisting that any landing in the Normandy region would represent only a diversion. Hitler, along with Rundstedt, had by then become convinced that the main Allied assault would strike north of the Somme.

On June 5, Rommel left his headquarters in France, planning to meet with Hitler the next day in Berchtesgaden. He hoped to persuade the Führer to transfer two additional armored divisions and another mortar brigade to Normandy. But it was too late.

D Day: The Air Drops

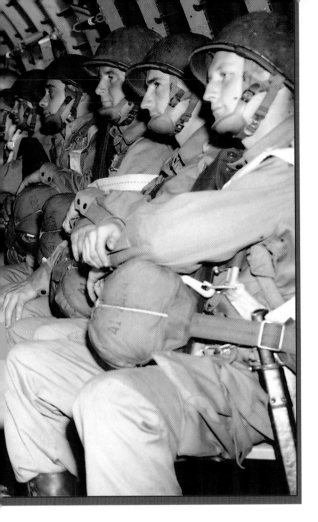

Each man loaded with his own set of equipment, paratroopers fly towards France as the first wave of the Allied invasion. The necessary equipment also turned out to be a death sentence for some; many paratroopers were so weighted down that they drowned in just a few feet of water.

"Lord, Thy will be done. But if I'm to die please help me to die like a man."

—Sergeant Elmo Jones, 505th Parachute Infantry Regiment, just before jumping into Normandy, June 6, 1944

On the night of June 5, 1944, Percy Wallace, a lighthouse keeper, watched the gathering of a vast armada off St. Gibans Head, England. Turning to his wife, he asked her to kneel with him. "A lot of men are going to die tonight," he said. "We should pray for them."

About 10 miles inland in southwestern England, at an

airstrip at Uppottery, U.S. paratroopers of Easy Company, 505th Parachute Infantry Regiment (PIR), 82nd Airborne Division, assembled in hangars in plane-load groups of 18 at 8:30 that same night. Each jump master (group leader) read a message to his troopers from their supreme commander. General Dwight D. Eisenhower's message said: "Soldiers, Sailors and Airmen of the Allied Expeditionary Force! You are about to embark upon the Great Crusade, toward which we have striven these many months. The eyes of the world are upon you. . . . Good Luck! And let us all beseech the blessing of Almighty God upon this great and noble undertaking."

At 10:00 P.M., the jump masters called for mount-up and pushed their charges up the steps of their waiting C-47 Dakotas, the military version of the venerable Douglas DC-3 airliner. From the door of one C-47, a lone trooper turned and faced east. Speaking for all of his 13,400 companions in the U.S. 82nd and 101st Airborne Divisions, he shouted, "Look out, Hitler! Here we come!" At 11:10 P.M., the C-47s started rumbling down the runway and taking to the air.

Twenty minutes later, a converted Short Stirling bomber of the Royal Air Force's 38 Group roared off the runway at RAF Keevil. It bore elements of the 12th Yorkshire Parachute Battalion of the British 6th Airborne Division. Winging toward Normandy, Captain Philip Burkinshaw experienced mixed emotions. Would they be dropped on or near their drop zone? Might foul weather conditions drive them well behind enemy lines? Would he find their rendezvous? How would he shape up as a platoon leader under fire and exposed to the unfamiliar horrors of war? Was he capable of the leadership that his men deserved? Mostly, the captain feared fear itself. "The moment of reckoning was inexorably approaching for me," Captain Burkinshaw noted later, "as it was for thousands of others in the air, on land and on sea."

Shortly after midnight on Tuesday, June 6, 1944, in the French town of Ste.-Mère-Église, Madame Angèle Levrault awakened to the reflections of flickering lights in her mirror. She heard the drone of aircraft engines throbbing and the muffled booming of explosions in the distance, followed by the staccato reports of rapid-firing antiaircraft batteries. Cherbourg, she assumed, was being bombed again. The 60-year-old schoolmistress felt thankful that she lived in a quiet town about 27 miles away. She donned her shoes and robe and walked across her flare-illuminated garden toward the detached outhouse.

The sound of approaching aircraft grew louder. Every flak battery—antiaircraft artillery units about the size of a company—in the district opened fire. Momentarily frightened, Madame Levrault dashed under a tree for cover as the planes roared overhead and the German guns thundered in violent protest. In another moment, the planes passed over, the engines faded, the guns ceased firing, and the garden fell back into silence. Suddenly a strange fluttering sound followed by a thud broke the stillness. An instant later, Private Robert M. Murphy fell head over jump boots into the old woman's garden. She stood frozen in fear at the sight of the gaunt 18-year-old with war paint on his face. He raised a finger to his lips in a gesture of silence and slipped away into the night.

Private Murphy was a pathfinder of the 82nd Airborne's 505th Regiment—one of the men who marked the drop zones with flares or electronic beacons in advance of the main airborne assault. Madame Levrault glanced at her watch. It was 12:15 A.M. She had just witnessed the arrival of one of the first Americans to land in Normandy.

■   ■   ■

The pathfinders of the three Allied airborne divisions went first, the vanguard of roughly 23,400 American and British paratroopers. About an hour later, the main assault forces followed. They dropped at both ends of the designated invasion beaches, code-named (from west to east) Utah, Omaha, Gold, Juno, and Sword. The British 6th Airborne Division jumped on the left (east) flank of the invasion site, east of the Orne River; the U.S. 82nd and 101st Airborne Divisions dropped on the right (west) flank, between Ste.-Mère-Église and Carentan on the Cotentin Peninsula.

British paratroopers were assigned the task of capturing the crossings over the Orne River and the Caen Canal to block the anticipated flow of German reinforcements. When the Germans realized that the main Allied invasion was taking place in Normandy rather than in Calais, they would most certainly rush reinforcements to the more weakly defended Normandy region. (At the time of the invasion, the Atlantic Wall in Normandy was only about 28 percent complete.)

A special glider-borne company of the British 6th Airborne Division had already captured one vital crossing over the Caen Canal at Bénouville. Major John Howard's D Company of the Oxfordshire and Buckinghamshire Light Infantry (or "Ox and Bucks") had flown in with the pathfinders and secured the bridge within 10 minutes. Their rapid conquest constituted the first secured objective of the invasion. (After the war, the crossing was dubbed "Pegasus Bridge" for the division's flying horse insignia. Pegasus is a winged horse from

Once on land, a force initially made up of 23,400 paratroopers advanced toward strategic water crossings, gun placements, and nearby towns. Women from Ste.-Marie-du-Mont greet liberating soldiers of the 101st Airborne early on June 7.

Greek mythology.) Most of the glider-borne troops of all three airborne divisions did not land in Normandy until later that morning.

Perhaps Lieutenant Colonel Terence Otway's 9th Parachute Battalion drew the 6th Division's toughest assignment. They were charged with silencing the heavily fortified German gun emplacement at Merville. Its heavy guns commanded the left flank of the British landing beaches. The divisional commander, Major

General Richard Gale, had instructed Otway, "Your attitude of mind must be that you cannot contemplate failure in the direct assault." Otway knew that Merville's big guns would slaughter any troops who might try to cross Sword Beach unless he and his men could put the guns out of action.

Otway's task seemed ill-fated from the start. First, five gliders bearing his antitank guns, jeeps, flamethrowers, mortars, and scaling ladders snapped their towlines and crashed into the English Channel. Then his pilots, zigzagging to avoid enemy flak, scattered his battalion of some 750 men across 50 square miles of Normandy. Miraculously, Otway somehow managed to round up about 155 of his widely dispersed troops and mount an attack on the big guns of Merville. Instead of surrounding the battery in battalion force, however, the 29-year-old major led a frontal assault. Savage, hand-to-hand combat ensued.

One group of paratroopers engaged the battery's machine gunners, while a second party stormed the concrete blockhouse, tossing grenades and emptying their weapons. Otway's reduced force—about one-fifth its original size—quickly overwhelmed the German gunners and destroyed their big guns with explosive charges. The assault lasted only 30 minutes. After it ended, Otway's signal officer pulled a carrier pigeon from his blouse and sent it winging back across the Channel with news that another vital objective of the 6th Airborne had been achieved.

The British had expected to incur high casualties during their nighttime airdrops on D Day. But their operations went better than expected. Such was not the case with their American counterparts to the west.

After pathfinder Robert Murphy encountered Madame Levrault in her garden, the young trooper had hurried off toward his drop zone near Ste.-Mère-Église. Moments later, he heard a short burst of gunfire to his right. Murphy did not find out until later that his buddy, Private Leonard Devorchak, had been shot at that instant. Devorchak had vowed to "win a medal a day just to prove to myself that I can make it." A German bullet ended his chance to earn a medal. And he became possibly the first American to be killed on D Day.

The mission of the U.S. 82nd and 101st Airborne Divisions—commanded by Major Generals Matthew B. Ridgway and Maxwell D. Taylor, respectively—was to seal off road exits from the invasion beaches and to seize key bridges and road junctions. Success in accomplishing their assignments would deny German access to the battlefield and open the way for the Allied armies to advance inland.

Much like their British brethren, the Americans jumped off to a poor start. The two American divisions ended up similarly scattered. Only one regiment—the 505th Parachute Infantry Regiment of the 82nd—fell accurately. Both divisions lost more than half of their equipment, including most of their radios, mortars, and ammunition. It would take the paratroopers hours, days, or, in a few cases, weeks to reunite with their units.

"Hundreds of men, heavily weighted with equipment, fell into the treacherous swamps of the Merderet and the Douve [Rivers]," wrote combat correspondent Cornelius Ryan. "Many drowned, some in less than two feet of water. Others, jumping too late, fell into the darkness over what they thought was Normandy and were lost in the Channel."

All over Normandy that night, paratroopers and German soldiers stumbled upon each another in accidental encounters that usually ended in capture or death for one or the other. Each paratrooper carried a dime-store cricket to use as a signaling device. A single *click-clack* squeeze called for a response of two: *click-clack, click-clack*. Some Germans stripped prisoners of their crickets and used them to lure more Americans into captivity. Despite the darkness and confusion, the paratroopers managed to reassemble in catch-as-catch-can fashion and achieve their aims.

About 1:45 A.M., at the headquarters of General of Artillery Erich Marcks's 84th Corps in St.-Lô, staff intelligence officer Major Friedrich Hayn received word of enemy parachute troops landing in three separate drop zones in Normandy. He reasoned that "they could, by attacking the strongpoints immediately west of the beach, paralyze the coastal defenses. If it really was the task of the reported enemy forces to keep open the crossings, it meant that an enemy landing would soon take place and they were really in earnest!" Hayn had reasoned correctly.

Fifteen minutes later, about 25 miles southeast of Caen, elements of Major General Edgar Feuchtinger's 21st Panzer Division stood with tank engines running, awaiting orders to move out. "We waited for orders, and we waited," *Gefreiter* (acting corporal) Werner Kortenhaus remembered later. "Just stood there, inactive by our tanks. We couldn't understand why we weren't getting any orders at all." Most German leaders still believed that the paratrooper activity was just a feint to divert German forces from a main attack soon to come at Calais.

At 3:00 A.M., not quite two hours after the arrival of the airborne troops, almost 2,000 medium and heavy Allied bombers commenced a two-hour preinvasion pummeling of the German defenses in the landing area. A naval bombardment followed, with the big guns of seven battleships, 18 cruisers, 43 destroyers, and two gunboats pounding the shoreline.

Gliders, special engineless planes capable of flying beneath enemy radar, carried troops, trucks, and small artillery. They were pulled part of the distance to France by conventional, engine-propelled planes with tow lines that sometimes broke. The advance forces the gliders carried helped diminish the Germans' ability to fend off the later, main invading effort.

Joseph Driscoll, war correspondent of the New York *Herald Tribune,* writing from aboard an Allied warship in the Channel, noted, "[H]ere we are crossing the water and the Germans, who once upon a time sang that they were sailing against England, are now cowering behind the Atlantic Wall, which our guns are pounding with a sound and fury like the worst storm multiplied a million."

At about 4:00 A.M., Private John Fitzgerald of the 101st, while scrambling across the Cotentin in the dark, bumped into a captain and a private from the 82nd. The trio joined forces and started looking for other troopers to add to their numbers. Right about then, the glider-borne troops began to arrive, and a German antiaircraft (AA) battery opened up on the gliders. "With all the noise, we were able to crawl to within twenty-five yards of the battery," Fitzgerald recounted.

The captain whispered brief attack orders. On cue, the private opened fire with his Browning automatic rifle (BAR), hitting two Germans on the right of the gun platform, while the captain tossed a grenade that exploded directly beneath the gun. "I emptied my M-1 [Garand semiautomatic rifle] clip [of eight rounds] at the two Germans on the left," Fitzgerald went on. "In a moment it was over. Perspiration broke out on my forehead, my hands were trembling. It was the first time I had ever fired at a living thing."

At approximately the same time, Lieutenant Colonel Ed Krause, of the 82nd's 3rd Battalion, 505th PIR, with about 180 paratroopers that he had reassembled, secured his objective: Ste.-Mère-Église. Villager Andre Mace, who had hidden in a garage during the brief but intense fighting for the town, wrote in his diary: "It is real hell all over with the firing of guns, machine guns, and artillery. At about 3:00 A.M. we risk a peek to see what is going on. The Americans are the only ones in the streets of the town, there are no more Germans. It is an indescribable joy." Ste.-Mère-Église had just become the first town in France to be liberated.

Shortly before sunrise, in German Seventh Army headquarters at Le Mans, chief of staff Major General Max Pemsel called his staff together in his well-lighted map room. In his usual calm, quiet voice that left only his words to convey the deep concern that he felt, he said, "Gentlemen, I am convinced the invasion will be upon us by dawn. Our future will depend on how we fight this day. I request of you all the effort and pain that you can give." At Army Group B headquarters in La Roche-Guyon, no one considered the situation critical enough yet to summon Field Marshal Erwin Rommel.

By daybreak, despite the time lost to scattered formations and related regrouping difficulties—not to mention the unfamiliar and hostile terrain—the men of the British and American airborne divisions had invaded the Continent and secured a foothold. Their positions remained precarious, and there was much fighting left to be done. But help was on the way.

Once out of the first deathtrap, the water, it was on to the next, the beach itself. American GIs pause to shelter below a concrete seawall before advancing over it to face the inevitable, successive line of German resistance. Nazi commanders knew the first 24 hours would be crucial in fending off an Allied invasion.

D Day:
The Beach Landings

"Believe me, Lang, the first twenty-four hours of the invasion will be decisive . . . the fate of Germany depends on the outcome . . . for the Allies, as well as Germany, it will be the longest day."

—Field Marshal Erwin Rommel to his aide,
Captain Hellmuth Lang, April 22, 1944

At 4:00 A.M. on June 6, 1944, while British and American paratroopers still struggled to complete their missions before sunrise, Allied warships steamed within range of German coastal guns along the Normandy shoreline. A naval bombardment group comprising the U.S. battleships *Texas*

(BB-35) and *Arkansas* (BB-33) knifed through the choppy waters of the Channel and took up station off the bluffs at Pointe du Hoc, the D Day objective of the U.S. 2nd and 5th Ranger Battalions. The point separated Utah and Omaha Beaches. Allied intelligence believed that German guns on the bluffs menaced both landing sites.

As dawn broke over the Channel, the Allied invasion fleet lined the entire horizon off Normandy from Caen to Vierville-sur-Mer. "They came, rank after relentless rank, ten lanes wide, twenty miles across, five thousand ships of every description," one reporter wrote that morning. The vast array of warships, cargo ships, troop transports, and landing craft of all shapes and sizes made up the greatest invasion fleet of all time.

Allied warships—battleships, light and heavy cruisers, destroyers and destroyer escorts, and the like—commenced firing their big guns at 5:50 A.M., detonating large German minefields and devastating many onshore block-houses and artillery installations. Captain Charles A. Baker, skipper of the *Texas,* shared the bridge of the "Big T" with task group commander Rear Admiral Carleton F. Bryant. The admiral's orders allowed no room for interpretation: "Push straight in and slug it out!"

Texas opened fire in unison with the other warships, unleashing salvo after fiery salvo against the German emplacements near the bluffs of Pointe du Hoc. For more than a half hour, the pre–World War I battleship's 14-inch guns pounded the enemy's six-foot-thick concrete-and-steel bunkers near the shore, while its 5-inch guns focused on fortified pillboxes behind the bluffs. Allied bombers had begun the bombardment of Pointe du Hoc weeks before D Day. The aging battleship picked up where the bombers had left off. All told, the Allies blasted the point with more than 10 kilotons of high explosives, nearly equal to the

Allied Order of Battle on D Day

SUPREME HEADQUARTERS ALLIED EXPEDITIONARY FORCE (SHAEF)
Supreme Commander: General Dwight D. Eisenhower
Deputy Supreme Commander: Air Chief Marshal Sir Arthur Tedder
Chief of Staff: Major General Walter Bedell Smith

21ST ARMY GROUP
General Sir Bernard L. Montgomery

U.S. 1ST ARMY
Lieutenant General Omar N. Bradley

5TH CORPS
Major General Leonard T. Gerow
1st Infantry Division
(Follow-up divisions: 2nd and 29th Infantry Divisions; 2nd Armored Division)

7TH CORPS
Major General J. Lawton Collins
4th Infantry Division
(Follow-up divisions: 9th, 79th, and 90th Infantry Divisions)

FOLLOW-UP CORPS
8th and 19th Corps

AIRBORNE
82nd and 101st Airborne Divisions
•

BRITISH 2ND ARMY
Lieutenant General Sir Miles Dempsey

1ST CORPS
Lieutenant General J. T. Crocker
3rd Infantry Division; Canadian 3rd Infantry Division
27th Armored Brigade; Canadian 2nd Armored Brigade
(Follow-up division: 51st Infantry Division)

30TH CORPS
General B. C. Bucknall
50th Infantry Division
8th Armored Brigade
(Follow-up divisions: 49th Infantry Division; 7th Armored Division)

FOLLOW-UP CORPS
8th and 12th Corps; Canadian 2nd Corps

AIRBORNE
6th Airborne Division

The U.S. battleship Texas was part of a bombardment that targeted German artillery at Normandy for two hours before the first infantry landed. Similar battleships also came to the rescue of American soldiers pinned down at Omaha Beach between the sea and enemy guns high up on overlooking cliffs.

explosive force of the atomic bomb used at Hiroshima.

While the guns of *Texas* softened the shore emplacements, the rangers boarded LCA vehicles and headed shoreward. (LCA stood for landing craft, assault; it was the British armor-added version of the basic boat design of American Andrew Higgins. The Higgins boat, as it was often called, was officially designated LCVP, or landing craft, vehicle, personnel. It was the workhorse of World War II amphibious operations.) *Texas* lifted fire at

6:30 A.M., timing its cessation with the rangers' scheduled arrival ashore. But the rangers were late, their flotilla of LCAs having been driven off course by the strong tidal current.

Meanwhile, cargo and troop-hauling vessels scurried about the choppy Channel waters in a rush to carry out the many tasks essential to landing troops and equipment on the shores of Normandy. These vessels comprised a virtual seafaring alphabet soup of landing ships and craft, with designations that included LSTs (landing ship, tank), LCTs (landing craft, tank), LCIs (landing craft, infantry), LBKs (landing barge, kitchen), and LCMs (landing craft, mechanized), along with LCAs, LCVPs, and a multitude of others. And trailing the warships, cargo ships, troopships, and landing craft, a host of Channel tugboats towed elements of the two MULBERRIES that would be assembled to form artificial harbors shortly after Allied troops secured a beachhead in Normandy.

"Amid the seething mass of men and ships, the throb of motors, the clank of landing craft against unyielding steel plates of the mother ships," writes Charles B. MacDonald, decorated combat veteran and later deputy chief historian of the Department of the Army, "big naval guns belched with such noise and vehemence toward the hostile shore that the ships appeared to rock deep in the water from the convulsive effort. Here and there angry coastal batteries tried to return the fire, but it was a one-sided duel." A single fleeting appearance by the German navy accomplished little.

Adds MacDonald: "From behind a smokescreen three German torpedo boats tried briefly but generally ineffectively to inflict some hurt. Only one found a mark, a Norwegian destroyer; thereupon the torpedo boats scurried back to base, thus ending the German navy's sole contribution to D Day."

The German air force contributed little more to aid the German cause on D Day, prompting one young GI (which stands for "government issue," slang for American soldier) to remark later, "We were all more or less expecting . . . dive bombers . . . continually backed by high level bombing. But no, nothing like that. . . . The Luftwaffe is obviously smashed." Hitler's air force managed fewer than 300 sorties (each sortie representing a single flight by a single aircraft) over the invasion area on D Day.

H hour was set at 6:30 A.M. Wave upon wave of landing craft of all descriptions formed offshore and headed for the beaches. The Allied master plan called for the U.S. 4th Infantry Division to land at Utah Beach on the Allied west or right flank (facing shoreward). To the left of the 4th and moving eastward along the invasion beaches, the U.S. ranger battalions were to come ashore at Pointe du Hoc; the U.S. 1st Infantry Division—the storied "Big Red One"—was to strike at Omaha; the British 50th Infantry Division, at Gold; the Canadian 3rd Division, at Juno; and the British 3rd, at Sword.

All of these divisions, as well as the Allied airborne divisions, came under the overall umbrella of the 21st Army Group, commanded by British general Sir Bernard L. Montgomery. His command was further broken down into the U.S. 1st Army (5th and 7th Corps) and the British 2nd Army (1st and 30th Corps). Each corps contained several divisions; for example, the U.S. 5th Corps was made up of the 1st, 2nd, and 29th Infantry Divisions and the 2nd Armored Division.

The Americans went in first with the U.S. 4th Division's 8th Infantry Regiment leading the way at Utah, followed by the 22nd and 12th Regiments. At the same time, the U.S. 2nd Ranger Battalion hit the beach at Pointe du Hoc, and the U.S. 1st Division's 16th and the 29th Division's 116th Regimental Combat Teams (RCTs) spearheaded the landings at Omaha, followed by the rest of the divisions. The master plan began to go awry when the landing craft arrived late, affording the Germans time to shore up their defenses.

By the time Lieutenant Colonel James E. Rudder's 2nd Ranger Battalion reached the beach, the Germans had rushed machine guns and mortars into the concrete-and-steel gun emplacements. "The Rangers caught hell," reported Lieutenant Weldon James, a marine public relations officer aboard the *Texas*. "Six of their landing craft were swamped or sunk by mortar barrage. And, when they finally reached the beach, they were met with a devastating crossfire."

But the elite soldiers recovered quickly. "Without ever contacting expected reinforcements from their flanks, Colonel Rudder's men gained their objectives within 34 hours after the landing," James went on. "Although heavily outnumbered, the Rangers fought the enemy from shell hole to shell hole from blasted pillbox to ruined casement through trenches, tunnels, and farmhouses."

Meanwhile, from an inland vantage point high in a church steeple at Ste. Marie-du-Mont, Colonel Frederick von der Heydte, commander of the German 6th Parachute Regiment and a veteran of the fighting in Poland, France, Russia, Crete, and North Africa, observed the American landing at Utah Beach. He could scarcely believe his eyes. "All along the beach," he related in a 1991 interview, "were these small boats, hundreds of them, each disgorging thirty or forty armed men. Behind them were the warships, blasting away with their huge guns, more warships in one fleet than anyone had ever seen before." Von der Heydte climbed down from the steeple and sped off on his motorcycle in search of artillery support.

Right about then, *Newsweek* magazine correspondent Kenneth Crawford landed on Utah Beach with the 4th Division's first wave of troops. He was wearing a watch given to him the previous Christmas in North Africa by the renowned war correspondent Ernie Pyle. Crawford would always remember the time of his landing in France, "because my wristwatch, guaranteed to be waterproof, shockproof, and otherwise indestructible, was nothing of the kind. It stopped at exactly 6:30 when I stumbled off a landing barge into four feet of water. The watch was nevermore to run." Crawford's wave had landed precisely at H Hour—but in the wrong place.

Brigadier General Theodore Roosevelt Jr., son of the late president and assistant division commander of the 4th Division, accompanied his infantrymen ashore in that same wave—the only general to arrive with the first wave of troops in Normandy on D Day. He saw at once that they were "not where we were supposed to be." They had landed about 2,000 yards south of their assigned location. The 53-year-old general faced a critical decision: Should he allow the succeeding waves to come ashore there or direct them farther up the beach? "We'll start the war from right here," he reportedly said. Despite an arthritic hip, Roosevelt spent the rest of the morning trudging up and down the fire-raked beach directing traffic.

Everything in combat is relative, of course, and compared with what was happening on Omaha Beach, the landings at Utah went well. The Americans quickly gained the upper hand. After about three hours of hard fighting, the German defenders surrendered the beach, and a steady flow of Allied troops and supplies began streaming inland. But if events at Utah Beach went well, the assault on Omaha Beach only narrowly averted disaster.

While the U.S. 2nd and 5th Ranger Battalions were

attacking Pointe du Hoc—to the west, or right, of Omaha Beach (facing the shore)—the 116th and 16th Regimental Combat Teams served as the vanguard for the landings at Omaha. Their troubles commenced from the moment they boarded their landing craft about 10 to 12 miles offshore— and grew steadily worse from there. Everything that could go wrong did, starting with seasickness.

Sergeant Benjamin McKinney, a combat engineer attached to C Company of the 116th RCT, later recalled that when the ramp of his landing craft dropped, "I was so seasick I didn't care if a bullet hit me between the eyes and got me out of my misery." A host of McKinney's fellow GIs shared a similar misery that morning, for the rough seas exacted a high toll from those unable to cope with the seafaring malady. And the price of passage through the choppy Channel waters mounted steadily on their shoreward journey.

In the first wave, 10 of the slab-sided landing craft capsized in the thrashing seas. Many of the 300 men aboard drowned. Innumerable DUKW amphibious trucks, called "ducks" after their acronym, also foundered. And of 96 DD (duplex drive) tanks fitted with flotation devices and called "swimming tanks," 57 went down. But those that "swam" ashore posed a fearsome sight for enemy eyes. Second Lieutenant Arthur Jahnke thought he was hallucinating when he first saw them at an exit from Utah Beach. "Amphibious tanks!" he recalled later. "This must be the Allies' secret weapon."

At the shoreline, adverse currents shoved many land- ing craft away from their assigned beach sectors. Omaha Beach was split into eight sectors, designated—from right to left (looking shoreward)—Charlie, Dog Green, Dog White, Dog Red, Easy Green, Easy Red, Fox Green, and Fox Red. The 116th RCT's sectors ran from Charlie to Easy Green, with the remaining three belonging to the

16th. Landing out of position rendered maps useless and deprived the invaders of friendly fire support from warships offshore.

Many men drowned when they stepped out of their boats too soon in water above their heads and were weighted down by their heavy gear. Others waded into underwater shell craters and drowned.

Allied bombing attacks and naval bombardments designed to soften the German positions proved ineffective. Heavy cloud cover obscured visibility. Bomber pilots, afraid of hitting friendly troops on the beaches, overshot their targets and dropped their bomb loads too far inland. And the accuracy of naval gunfire was diluted by the loss of radios used by onshore artillery spotters. Most of their radios went down with the landing craft that did not make it to the beaches.

Once ashore at Omaha, the GIs encountered a tangle of obstructions—concrete cones, slanted poles, logs tilted seaward with mines lashed to their tips, and steel rails welded together and set into the beach so that their ends would pierce the bottoms of landing craft. Behind the beach obstacles stood a line of cliffs some four miles long and 150 feet high, whose ravines and draws were strewn with antitank and antipersonnel mines. From strategically located blockhouses, bunkers, and machine-gun nests scattered in the bluffs above, mortar and artillery batteries of the highly disciplined German 352nd Infantry Division poured down destruction upon the attacking Americans. German machine guns raked the shore and decimated more than one-third of the first wave of attackers, some of whom were forced to wade in from 50 to 100 yards when their landing craft bottomed out on unseen sandbars.

Once ashore, the surviving GIs, lacking most of their heavy weapons, could only hunker down behind sand

Wounded troops of the U.S. 16th Infantry Regiment at Omaha Beach wait by the infamous cliffs to be taken to a field hospital. This sector experienced near-disaster when water currents threw landing troops out of positions; deadly obstacles littered the shoreline and beach; equipment was blown up by the enemy; and clouds obscured German guns from overhead bombers.

dunes and a low seawall that ran along the base of the beach. Many were killed in place. Others, wounded and unable to move, drowned when the tide moved in. When new waves of soldiers arrived, they merely contributed to the chaos, adding to the heaps of dead and huddled masses of surviving GIs. American casualties at Omaha would soon total one man wounded or killed for each square yard of beach.

Novelist and *Collier's* war correspondent Ernest Hemingway, arriving on Omaha with the seventh wave, reported: "The first, second, third, fourth and fifth waves lay where they had fallen, looking like so many heavily laden bundles on the flat pebbly stretch between the sea and the first cover." By midmorning, live GIs interspersed with the dead along the pebbled swath formed a motionless sash seven yards wide. And an incoming tide was beginning to reclaim the beach.

Although combat engineers and navy demolition units attempted to blast avenues of approach through the beach obstacles, their efforts returned only marginal successes. Of 16 bulldozers that landed intact, only 3 survived enemy fire, and GIs seeking shelter from incoming fire behind one of those restricted its freedom of movement. Still, the engineers and navy teams succeeded in opening six complete lanes, but not without paying a stiff price. The engineers sustained 40 percent casualties, most coming within the first half hour of the attack. But the relentless German fire continued to keep the GIs in place.

Offshore, aboard the heavy cruiser *Augusta*, U.S. 1st Army commander Lieutenant General Omar N. Bradley was experiencing "a time of grave personal anxiety and frustration" stemming from an almost total lack of communication with his assault troops on Omaha Beach. The few messages that reached him led him to believe that "our forces had suffered an irreversible catastrophe." Bradley would later reveal that he "considered evacuating the beachhead and directing the follow-up troops to Utah Beach or the British beaches."

Above Omaha Beach, an elated Lieutenant General Dietrich Kraiss, commander of the German 352nd Infantry Division, felt certain that the American assault was faltering. Accordingly, he shifted some of his reserves to the east, where he perceived the British as representing the greater threat.

The British 50th Infantry and Canadian 3rd Infantry Divisions splashed ashore on Gold and Juno Beaches at 7:25 A.M., some 55 minutes after the American landings on Utah and Omaha. Ten minutes later, the British 3rd Infantry Division landed on Sword, the easternmost beach. (Tide variations dictated the differences in landing times.) Allied planning called for a rapid armored break-through of the German front, seizure of the critical road junctions at Bayeux and Caen, a quick linkup with the paratroopers east of the Orne River, and a speedy joining of the Allied beachheads. Montgomery expected the British forces to capture Caen, 32 miles inland, by night-fall—an ambitious aim at best.

Initially, the British 50th Division came under heavy fire from Lieutenant General Wilhelm Richter's German 716th Infantry Division on Gold. But the British troops soon planted themselves ashore and pushed inland without great difficulty. The Canadian 3rd fared similarly well. Instead of the high bluffs and sharp banks that the American troops faced at Omaha, the British forces found gently shelving beaches with small summer resorts strung out along a coastal road. Nonetheless, the pastoral setting provided a backdrop for plenty of action for the invaders.

When the 47th Royal Marine commandos churned toward shore at Gold Beach, German defenders sank 4 of their 16 landing craft and severely damaged 11 others. Only one made it back to its parent vessel. Sergeant Donald Gardner of the 47th—dumped in the water with his men about 50 yards from shore and forced to swim the rest of the way under heavy machine-gun fire—heard one of his men say, "Perhaps we're intruding, this seems to be a private beach."

Canadians and British encountered less enemy resistance and easier terrain at the eastern beaches of Gold, Juno, and Sword. Their landing was delayed due to differing high tides, however, and their attack lacked the element of surprise. Here, troops of the Canadian 3rd Division leave a ship with bicycles to help them move inland and conquer their next military objective: the town of Caen 32 miles inland.

At Juno, troops of the Canadian 3rd Infantry Division and British support units met stiff German resistance. They had to choose between being gunned down in place or advancing through uncleared mine fields at the risk of being blown up. Grant Suche, a 22-year-old rifleman with the Canadian Royal Winnipeg Rifles, would never forget the sight that greeted the Rifles on Juno: "The first thing we saw were bodies, and parts of bodies, our own people, and this country that was strange to us, and all these pill boxes everywhere. . . . I can always remember seeing the steeple of this church, and there were snipers up there zapping us with lead flying all around." The Canadians chose to hammer their way off the beach, which they did with resolution and dispatch.

To the left (east) of the Canadians lay Sword Beach, at the mouth of the Orne, the last beach of the Allied assault. German defenders offered mixed resistance to the men of the British 3rd Infantry Division, generally light except at the eastern end of the narrow beach. To the astonishment of Captain Gerald Norton of a British artillery unit, he was met "by four Germans with their suitcases packed, who appeared to be awaiting the first available transportation out of France."

The landings at Sword went well initially, with the 3rd Division's entire assault brigade making it ashore by 9:43 A.M., only 18 minutes behind schedule. At this point, however, clearing the beach exits became sticky, and the narrowness of the beach became a factor as troops and equipment began piling up on the slender frontage. The beach congestion allowed time for German gunners to play havoc with the pileup. And the weather, mines, obstacles, and enemy shelling combined to cause significant losses of landing craft. In spite of the ensuing disarray, the British—using American Sherman and British Churchill tanks and their .50-caliber machine guns and 75mm cannon to blast new paths— finally cleared the exits and started advancing inland. But Montgomery's D Day timetable fell far behind, jeopardizing his expectation of seizing Caen by day's end.

Meanwhile, after clinging to the beaches for three hellish hours on Omaha, the Americans remained pinned down and in danger of being driven back into the sea. Just

Unbelievable heroism took place on Normandy's soil in June 1944, also unbelievable tragedy. American corpses lie covered, awaiting burial, after the D Day invasion. As Dwight Eisenhower, then-Supreme Allied Commander, later said, "To think of the lives that were given, paying a terrible price on this beach alone."

before 10:00 A.M., U.S. 1st Division commander Major General Clarence R. Huebner interrupted the flow of matériel ashore and sent in troop reinforcements. And he called on naval gunners to knock out the German guns at the risk of hitting his own GIs.

Admiral Bryant obliged. "Get on them, men! Get on

them!" he radioed his destroyers. "They're raising hell with the men on the beach! We must stop them!" His destroyers flashed into action, sweeping in so close to shore that their keels occasionally scraped bottom. Back and forth they dashed in front of the beach, registering countless salvos on the vital exits and enemy gun positions for the next several hours. The destroyers delivered almost the only direct artillery support the GIs got while on the beach that day.

After Bryant's "tin cans" joined the fray, the battle slowly began to turn. At 11:00 A.M., Colonel George A. Taylor, commander of the 16th RCT, rallied his troops. "Two kinds of people are staying on this beach, the dead and those who are going to die," he shouted across his huddled ranks. "Now let's get the hell out of here!" Then, waving his men forward, Taylor led their attack into the jaws of the entrenched Germans.

And the Germans waited behind their guns.

The battle over the beach, itself, was over in 7 hours, but the battle of the bocage (or hedgerows), raged for weeks. The impressive Allied supply system, well noted by the Germans, included amphibious tanks and other armored vehicles that could be replaced almost daily. Barrage balloons float over ships off shore waiting to unload reinforcement supplied 12 days after the invasion.

The Beachhead: Moving In, Building Up, and Moving Out

"Troops formerly pinned down on beaches Easy Red, Easy Green, Fox Red [sectors of Omaha Beach] advancing up heights behind beaches."

—Major General Leonard T. Gerow,
U.S. 5th Corps commander, in his message to
U.S. 1st Army commander General Omar N. Bradley,
June 6, 1944, 1:09 P.M.

Pinpointing precisely when the blood-tinged tide of battle started turning in favor of the Americans on Omaha is at least in part a function of individual perspective. But it seems clear that the devastating naval gunfire brought to bear on German positions by Admiral Bryant's destroyers had a lot to do with turning things around, as this action report of the U.S. destroyer *Harding* indicates: "At 1050 observed enemy pillbox which was firing on troops down draw north of Colleville, thereby delaying operations on the beach. Opened fire on pillbox and demolished it, expending 30 rounds."

Meanwhile, German reaction to the Normandy landings had been incredibly slow at the highest level. Since early morning, General of Artillery Erich Marcks had been phoning almost continuously from 84th Corps headquarters to Seventh Army (Colonel General Friedrich Dollmann), to Army Group (Rommel), and even to OKW chief of staff Colonel General Alfred Jodl at Hitler's alpine hideaway at Berchtesgaden. "I need every available armored unit for a counterattack," he appealed to them.

OB West commander General Field Marshal Gerd von Rundstedt—still uncertain that Normandy was the great invasion—finally ordered two panzer divisions to move up but sent one to Deauville on the Pas de Calais. Jodl promptly countermanded the order. Rundstedt, furious, spent the rest of D Day morning pruning roses at his headquarters in St. Germain. Jodl, believing the situation in Normandy to be insufficiently developed to waken the late-sleeping Hitler, waited until 10:00 A.M. to rouse him. Hitler belatedly told Rundstedt that he could shift two panzer divisions to Normandy but no more. Rundstedt fumed in frustration. "His anger made his speech unintelligible," his aides said.

Word of the invasion reached Army Group B commander General Field Marshal Erwin Rommel at 10:15 A.M. at his home in Herrlingen, Bavaria, where he had been celebrating his wife's birthday. "I was right all along, all along," he repeated to his aide, Captain

Hellmuth Lang, during their speedy return to group headquarters in France.

Rommel had predicted that the battle for France would be won in the first 24 hours. And the Germans might have won it had they rushed three available panzer divisions into action during the early hours of D day. The combined force of the 12th SS and the 21st Panzer Divisions, along with the Panzer Lehr Division, might well have been sufficient to drive the Allies back into the sea in those first critical hours. But Hitler refused to commit them in time to make a difference. Although Rommel did not know it at the time, his forces had already lost the battle for Normandy's beaches while he was still motoring back to La Roche-Guyon.

While Rommel was speeding back to Normandy, Associated Press correspondent Don Whitehead was witnessing another example of the deadly effectiveness of destroyer gunnery. "The firepower of the navy was one of our salvations in those first few hours," he wrote, after watching a U.S. destroyer knock out a German blockhouse overlooking Easy Red. German gunners manning an 88mm gun had been "firing at almost point-blank range at the landing craft and the troops trapped at the edge of the water." An army-navy beach team radioed a destroyer for help and the tin can came racing in and neutralized the blockhouse with four well-placed rounds. Brigadier General Willard Wyman, assistant division commander of the Big Red One, then moved off the beach and set up his command post in the blockhouse. Whitehead wrote his first story of the landing there. "As I saw it," he recounted later, "that was when the battle of the beach was won—seven hours after the first wave hit the beach."

Notwithstanding the enormous contributions of Bryant's destroyers and an almost infinite number and variety of other support elements, when the last words are written about how the Americans won the day at Omaha Beach, one word will dominate the rest: infantry. At Normandy, as history has consistently demonstrated, it fell to the common foot soldier to turn apparent defeat into convincing victory. And it took leaders like Colonel Charles Canham, commander of the 116th RCT, who urged his men forward, shouting, "They're murdering us here. Let's move inland and get murdered"; or leaders like Captain Joe Dawson, commander of the 116th's G Company, whose clear, crisp orders were impossible to misconstrue. "Men, there is the enemy," he said, as he and his company advanced inland. "Let's go get them." For every yard of ground gained that day, there was an infantryman with an extraordinary tale to tell.

When the destroyers lifted fire, the German 352nd Division answered back with a series of counterattacks, all of them beaten off by the GIs, aided by newly arriving U.S. tanks and fresh reinforcements. The 352nd expended most of its reserves in unsuccessful attempts to dislodge the U.S. Rangers from Point du Hoc, which anchored the western (right) flank of Omaha. Finally, in early afternoon, elements of Major General Leonard T. Gerow's 5th Corps moved off the beach and began advancing up the heights. Shortly after 1:00 P.M., Gerow radioed 5th Corps' progress to his superior aboard *Augusta*.

General Bradley, who had been on the verge of withdrawing his beleaguered 1st Army troops on Omaha Beach and shifting them to the more stable environment of Utah Beach, took heart from Gerow's status report. "The situation everywhere on the beach was still grave," Bradley wrote later, "but our troops . . . were inclining inland. . . . I gave up any thought of abandoning Omaha Beach."

When darkness finally—and mercifully—ended the

first day's fighting, 5th Corps (1st and 29th Divisions) was clinging to a slender beachhead six miles long and not more than a mile and a half deep at Omaha. Fifth Corps had landed 34,000 troops and a huge volume of supplies and equipment on the day. Their losses totaled 2,500 dead and wounded. And much of their matériel lay wrecked and burning on the battle-ravaged beach. But they had broken through the hard crust of the German defenses in an inch-by-inch frontal assault and pressed forward to St. Laurent, Colleville, and Vierville. On this tiny beachhead—bloodied, battered, and exhausted—they welcomed the coming of night.

On Utah, Major General J. Lawton Collins's 7th Corps (4th Division) finished the day with fewer than 200 casualties. More than 20,000 troops and roughly 1,700 vehicles came ashore at Utah on D Day. The 4th Division moved inland around midday and started linking up with the U.S. airborne divisions on the Cotentin Peninsula that afternoon.

To the east, on Gold, Juno, and Sword, the British and Canadians forfeited any chance of surprising the Germans when forced by the tides to land slightly later than the Americans. Moreover, German fortifications and strongpoints along the three beaches survived the preliminary Allied bombardment. As a result, Lieutenant General Sir Miles Dempsey's British 2nd Army forces met strong German resistance at several points in the beginning. Unlike the Americans, however, they managed to land with Major General Sir Percy Hobart's armor and the Funnies—the general's specially modified tanks and armored vehicles for clearing beach obstacles, minefields, and so on—intact. Tank support and the aid of the beach-clearing Funnies enabled Dempsey's forces to fight their way off Gold and Juno beaches by morning's end and off Sword by late afternoon. (The British relied heavily on

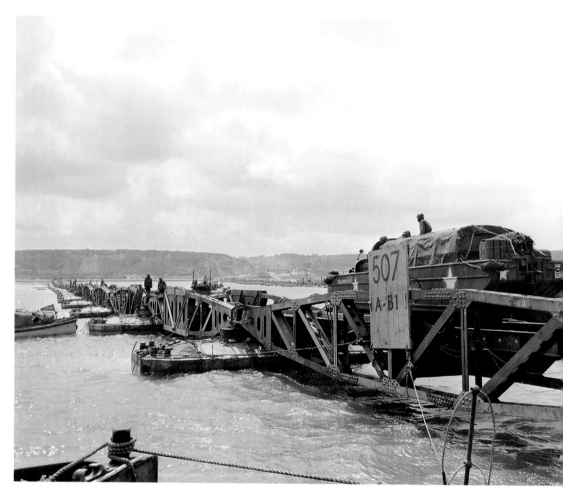

A MULBERRY, or extensive floating harbor, was used to support the Allied invasion. Two were put in place, one at each end of the line of five beaches. The Mulberry at Omaha was later destroyed by the powerful channel storms for which this part of France is known. Another innovation, the British Funnies, vehicles that clear beaches of armaments, also proved quite effective during this battle.

the Funnies and rather hoped that the Americans would see their value and use them. But the Americans preferred to use their own equipment—bulldozers and the like—a decision for which they took considerable criticism.)

Combined casualties for British-Canadian forces on

D Day totaled 4,100. They did not achieve Montgomery's perhaps overly ambitious goal of capturing Caen and would not for some time longer. By day's end, however, they had landed some 75,250 on their three beaches and stood firmly ensconced on French soil.

Rommel's so-called longest day ended with the Allies holding firm to a beachhead stretching some 55 miles. They had paid for the Normandy real estate with the blood of 9,000 casualties—half of them on Omaha Beach—but they had penetrated the Führer's vaunted Atlantic Wall in a single day. German losses remain unknown to this day but are thought to have been substantially higher.

In all, the landings had gone far better than Allied planners had expected. More than 100,000 men had come ashore in Normandy on D Day—the vanguard of millions to follow—along with untold tons of weaponry, vehicles, and matériel. But the Allied battle to take back Europe from Hitler was just beginning.

On D Day +1 (June 7), the invasion entered its second critical phase. The Allies concentrated first on linking up their four beachheads—Gold and Juno were already consolidated—so that they could expand farther inland to create room for the reinforcements and additional tonnages of matériel already starting to arrive. They began building up and moving out across the open country beyond the beaches simultaneously.

One GI scout fresh off Utah Beach met Sergeant Thomas Bruff, a paratrooper from the 101st, and asked, "Where's the war?" Bruff, not given to overstatement, replied, "Keep going, buddy. You'll find it."

From the German perspective, the Normandy landings had come as a total surprise. And it soon became clear to them that the Allies had come to stay. Lieutenant General Hans Speidel, Rommel's chief of staff, later acknowledged, "The first phase of the invasion ended with an obvious military, political, and psychological success for the Allies. . . . From June 9 on, the initiative lay with the Allies."

When Rundstedt and Rommel advised Hitler of the seriousness of the German military situation, the Führer silenced them and echoed his oft-repeated command: hold at all costs. They would try, but their armies were less than immovable objects. And the Allies, even as they gathered their dead for shipment back to England, were rapidly building an irresistible force.

The MULBERRIES arrived on D+1 and were sunk (positioned) off Omaha Beach and Gold Beach at St. Laurent and Arromanches, respectively. These artificial harbors were to serve until proper ports such as Cherbourg and Brest could be captured and made operational. (A gale would destroy the MULBERRY at Omaha on June 19, but the one at Gold remained in use until December 1944.) Allied plans called for the MULBERRIES to handle 25 divisions with all their equipment and mountains of matériel in the next three weeks. By sundown of D+10, 557,000 troops, 81,000 vehicles, and 183,000 tons of supplies had been brought ashore at the now thriving supply depots at Omaha and Gold.

One German divisional commander in Normandy, reporting on the American supply system, wrote: "I cannot understand these Americans. Each night we know that we have cut them to pieces, inflicted heavy casualties, mowed down their transport. But in the morning, we are suddenly faced with fresh battalions, with complete replacements of men, machines, tools, and weapons. This happens day after day."

Furthermore, Hitler's fixation with the notion that the Allies would mount another main-force invasion at Calais sorely hindered the defense strategy of Rundstedt and

German command was slow to react to the Normandy invasion, believing it to be only a diversion from the real, upcoming invasion to take place northeast of Calais. Here at Normandy 6 days after D Day, low tide reveals a landscape still cluttered with debris and the obstructions planted in the water by the Germans to hinder landing vehicles.

Rommel. German reinforcements arrived at the actual battle scene in bits and pieces, and piecemeal counter-attacks frittered away part of their panzer strength. "Since Hitler had the last say, one would have hoped that experts were consulted," noted panzer group commander General Geyr von Sweppenburg after the war, referring

A German cement gun turret overlooks the sands where the Allies lost 9,000 men in their valiant effort to take the beach. The artillery emplacement was quiet after being captured by Canadian troops who used the heavy scaling ladder to overcome the surrounding mass of barbed wire. The ladder was just one piece of equipment the infantry brought with them from the landing craft.

to Hitler's orders to move two reserve panzer divisions to the front during daylight hours, a reversal of his earlier orders. "This was not the case." Allied fighter-bombers decimated the panzers.

At the same time, however, treacherous terrain features aided the Germans, as American forces grappled with Normandy's treacherous *bocage*—a belt of higher ground that runs across the base of the Cotentin Peninsula in western France. The belt is marked by steep valleys, wooded hills, and crisscrossing narrow lanes bordered by high hedges. Each hedgerow served as a natural barrier infested with German machine-gun nests and antitank guns. The Allied advance soon slowed to a crawl, with German resistance centering on Carentan in the American sector and on Caen in the British zone.

On June 12, Collins's U.S. 7th Corps (Utah) overran Carentan and linked up with Gerow's U.S. 5th Corps (Omaha). The 7th then battered its way across the base of the Cotentin Peninsula, swung north, and captured Cherbourg on June 27. Although it would not become operational for two more months, the Allies now owned a proper port.

Three days later, on the last day of June, Operation NEPTUNE—the initial attack phase of Operation OVERLORD—officially ended.

Two French children watch Allied vehicles drive through the almost completely destroyed town of St.-Lô en route to the front. General Patton was moved from the mock invasion operation in Dover, England, to take over Operation COBRA and speed Allied advancement after taking this town. The Germans positioned only two panzer units to try to stop this operation.

Operation COBRA: Breakthrough at St.-Lô

"Now we are pinning our hopes on Bradley's attack. . . . We must go forward shoulder to shoulder, with honors and sacrifices equally shared."

—General Dwight D. Eisenhower, in a letter to General Sir Bernard L. Montgomery, July 1944

July started in a stalemate. The Americans now controlled the Cotentin Peninsula but still faced determined resistance from approximately seven veteran divisions of SS general Paul Hauser's Seventh Army. (Hauser replaced Dollmann, who had died of a heart attack on June 30.) The British and Canadians stood halted on an irregular line to the north of Caumont, Villers-Bocage, and Caen, barred from advancing further by seven armored and two infantry divisions of the Fifth Panzer Army (formerly Panzer Group West) under General Heinrich Eberbach (the Führer's replacement for Geyr von Schweppenburg).

In the American sector, the hedgerows—some higher than five feet and equally wide—plagued the GIs every step of the way. Allied planners, anticipating a German delaying action and retreat along the Seine, had paid little attention to the encumbrances imposed by the *bocage*. Corporal Bill Preston recalled the American situation this way: "We were stuck. . . . The whole theory of mobility that we had been taught, of our racing across the battlefield, seemed to have gone up in smoke."

Scripps-Howard correspondent Ernie Pyle described fighting in the hedgerows in more grisly terms: "This hedge to hedge stuff is a type of warfare we've never run into before, and I've seen more dead Germans than ever in my life. Americans too, but not nearly so many as the Germans. One day I'll think I'm getting hardened to dead people, dead young people in vast numbers, and then next day I'll realize I'm not and never could be." (An official army survey taken in portions of the rifle companies of the 1st, 4th, 9th, and 25th Infantry Divisions revealed that they lost almost 60 percent of their enlisted men and more than 68 percent of their officers between June 6 and July 31, 1944.)

Although the fall of Cherbourg represented a welcome victory, the Allies were in no position to rest for long on their laurels. Despite having landed about a million men and 177,000 vehicles in Normandy by July, their lodgment remained modest, extending inland for 25 miles at best but for little more than five miles in most places. Even so, the modest gains lifted Allied spirits and inversely lowered German morale.

Hitler, unhappy and exasperated over Rundstedt's continuing qualms and requests to withdraw to more defensible positions, relieved the old Prussian and replaced him as Commander in Chief West with Field Marshal Günther von Kluge on July 2. Kluge undertook his new assignment with great optimism. "At the start he was very cheerful and confident—like all newly appointed commanders," noted his chief of staff, General Günther Blumentritt. "Within a few days he became very sober and quiet. Hitler did not like the changing tone of his reports." Kluge's reports would grow steadily more pessimistic.

The decisive battle for Caen commenced on July 7 with the saturation bombing of the unfortunate town by 467 heavy bombers dropping 2,500 tons of explosives. On July 8 General Dempsey's British 2nd Army attacked with 115,000 men. Hitler ordered the city to be defended to the last man, but SS *Oberführer* (a rank between colonel and brigadier general) Kurt "Panzer" Meyer, commander of the 12th SS Panzer Division, ignored the order and fell back south of the Orne that night. "We were meant to die in Caen, but one just couldn't watch those youngsters being sacrificed to a senseless order," Meyer said. British and Canadian troops captured the city on July 9. Shortly thereafter, the Germans again halted their advance in the east.

On July 17, the fortunes of war claimed Field Marshal Rommel as a victim. Two British Spitfire fighter planes machine-gunned his open touring car and ran it into a ditch while the Army Group B commander was returning to his headquarters after inspecting his defenses. Rommel incurred severe head injuries and was forced to return to Germany. Kluge assumed his duties and Rommel took no further part in the Normandy campaign.

The next day, Montgomery launched Operation GOODWOOD, a major British-Canadian armored push aimed at the high ground east of Caen. Monty had indicated to Eisenhower that GOODWOOD might produce "far-reaching results," but only if backed by "the whole weight" of Allied airpower. Eisenhower interpreted Monty's comments as meaning a break-through—at last—in the Caen sector. Eisenhower obliged Monty and sent more than 2,200 planes to drop more than 7,000 tons of bombs to soften the avenues of Monty's attack.

On that same day, American GIs of the 29th Division, who had inched their way through the *bocage*, crunched on into St.-Lô in the west. New men joined their units at night in the middle of the battle, unknown to others by sight or name. Sometimes, a new arrival would die before dawn. "[W]ithout the sustain-ing strength of unit pride or comradeship," one officer of the 29th later wrote, "he had started battle reduced to the final resource with which every man ends it: himself." The Americans took 11,000 casualties in capturing St.-Lô.

After the fall of St.-Lô, a week of bad weather, contin-ued stiff German resistance, and negative terrain features combined to render further American advances impossible. The American offensive ground to a halt in the *bocage* once again. And the Allied timetable fell further behind. By then, however, U.S. 1st Army commander Omar Bradley had worked out a plan designed to achieve the illusive breakthrough. Bradley called his plan Operation COBRA. He cautioned his staff that COBRA required quick and decisive execution, or "we go right back to this hedge fighting and you can't make any speed. This thing must be bold."

Operation COBRA, according to Bradley, called for

The enormous victories of June 1944 would be followed by the stalemate of July 1944. The dense hedgerows of Normandy's bocage, or higher ground, provided excellent coverage for retreating German troops on the defense. This thick growth almost proved to be too much for the American forces making their way to Cherbourg.

"a place where you would not be hung up by swamps or river crossings. You wanted a terrain where there was a good road net so that you could use maximum troops and one from which you could break out on the other side and have a good road net to go in different directions after you had broken through the crust of German resistance." Bradley chose the St.Lô–Périers–Lessay Road. And he selected Lieutenant General George S. Patton—now in France and in command of the *real* U.S. 3rd Army—to spearhead the attack.

In the meantime, Operation GOODWOOD succeeded in chewing up four German divisions but failed to achieve a breakthrough in the Caen sector. It petered out on July 20. One of Montgomery's aides hastily informed Britain's War Office in London that the operation's main purpose had been "to muck up and write off the enemy troops," thus distracting German attention from COBRA. GOODWOOD did indeed draw off German forces from the St.-Lô sector, but whether that had been Montgomery's intent remains an issue for battle buffs to argue. In any case, when Bradley launched COBRA five days later, only two panzer divisions confronted him, as opposed to seven panzer divisions and four heavy tank battalions manning the German defense line east of Caen.

Also on July 20, an attempt was made to assassinate Hitler at his Rastenburg lair. The attempt failed when a bomb only slightly wounded the Führer. Lieutenant Colonel Claus Schenk von Stauffenberg, of the German general staff, and hundreds of other alleged conspirators were subsequently executed. Rommel, implicated in the plot, was forced to commit suicide. Poison—rather than shot or shell—ended the illustrious career of the Desert Fox.

COBRA began on July 25 with a massive saturation bombing of the area by more than 3,000 planes, including 1,500 heavy bombers of the U.S. 8th Air Force. The bombing pattern left crater-free lanes for the tanks that would follow. However, as a result of poor visibility and Germans firing American flares to misdirect the bombers, some of the bombs landed short, killing 111 GIs and wounding 490 others. The dead included Lieutenant General Lesley McNair, one of the principal aides of U.S. Army chief of staff General George C. Marshall. Bombs grant no privileges of rank. Only Bradley, Patton, and three others attended his funeral. Patton noted in his diary: "No band. A sad ending and useless sacrifice."

Collins's U.S. 7th Corps headed the main attack just west of St.-Lô, with Major General Troy H. Middleton's 8th Corps on their right. Despite the bombing catastrophe, the two corps made good progress. In a few days, Collins found his progress essentially unimpeded—and with good reason.

When the American attack commenced, Field Marshal Kluge sent a message to Lieutenant General Fritz Bayerlein, ordering him to hold the line. Bayerlein's Panzer Lehr Division, facing Collins's corps, had all but disappeared under the massive bombing attack. Bayerlein sent a scathing reply to OB West headquarters: "Out in the front every one is holding out. . . . Every one. . . . Not a single man is leaving his post. Not one! They're lying in their foxholes mute and silent, for they are dead. Dead! Do you understand? You may report to the field marshal [Kluge] that the Panzer Lehr Division is annihilated."

On July 27, Collins's 2nd Armored Division—the "Hell on Wheels" division—fought through a determined force of the 2nd SS Panzer and 17th SS Panzer Grenadier (armored infantry) to open country near St.-Denis-le-Gast. After the bloody battle one American officer described the carnage as "the most Godless sight I have ever witnessed on any battlefield." The next day, 7th Corps seized Coutances after advancing 12 miles in under three days.

Similar to the Normandy beaches, the peaceful western French countryside
became an impromptu battlefield strewn with dead German soldiers and
cattle. All was not quiet at military headquarters in Germany either.
An assassination attempt on Hitler failed and hundreds of his officers
were implicated, including Rommel (his one time favorite), who
committed suicide.

On July 28, Bradley decided that the time was right
to turn Patton loose. The twin towns of Avranches
and Pontaubault now represented the key to American
success in Normandy. They formed a "corner" that, once
turned, would open a gateway to an Allied advance into

Brittany and southern Normandy. Two days later, with Patton in overall command, Middleton's 8th Corps spearheaded the American drive and ripped a funnel-shaped hole in the German defenses, 10 miles wide at Avranches, narrowing to a single road and the bridge at Pontaubault. Patton told Middleton to cross the bridge "now!" Middleton did—and the gates to all of France flew open.

On August 1, Lieutenant General George S. Patton's U.S. 3rd Army became officially operational. With their breakthrough at St.-Lô, nothing remained to stop the Americans and their allies from entering Brittany. They left the hedgerows of the *bocage* behind and commenced a series of lightning thrusts that would carry them well down the road to Berlin—with Patton leading the way.

"In August 1944," writes Carlo D'Este, a Patton biographer, "his name and that of Third Army would be emblazoned in headlines across the world." And so they were.

Patton's 79th Infantry Division crossed the Seine during the night of August 19, the first Allied crossing of the fabled river. By August 25—D+80—the four Allied armies had closed in to the river, 10 days ahead of the 90-day time frame specified in the OVERLORD plan. General Charles de Gaulle's Free French forces liberated Paris on that same day. August 25 effectively marked the end of the Normandy campaign.

Symbolically, however, the campaign for Normandy did not end until General Eisenhower assumed command of the Allied ground forces on September 1, and General Montgomery was promoted to field marshal (to soothe his ruptured ego for having been replaced by Ike). The Normandy invasion and subsequent drive across France cost the Allies some 40,000 killed, 165,000

French General de Gaulle liberated Paris on August 25, 1944. Four days later, soldiers from Pennsylvania's 28th Infantry Division marched along the main boulevard, the Camps Elysees, with the Arc de Triomphe in the background. But World War II would not be over for more than a year, with Germany surrendering on May 7, 1945.

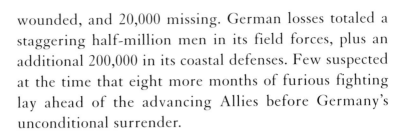

wounded, and 20,000 missing. German losses totaled a staggering half-million men in its field forces, plus an additional 200,000 in its coastal defenses. Few suspected at the time that eight more months of furious fighting lay ahead of the advancing Allies before Germany's unconditional surrender.

Two decades after D Day, former President Eisenhower returned to Omaha Beach to pay tribute to the soldiers who died that day to keep the U.S. and its Allies free. He also toured St. Laurent cemetery where thousands of U.S. soldiers are buried; it's one site in France that is frequently visited by Americans. How would world history have been affected if Ike had postponed the invasion that dark and stormy night?

Aftermath: What Free Men Will Do

"It [the Normandy campaign] was one terrible blood-letting."

—Field Marshal Erwin Rommel,
commander, German Army Group B

During the rest of the summer and fall of 1944, the Allied armies battled across the north of France and northwest Europe, mounted a second invasion on the south coast of France (Operation DRAGOON), and settled in along the West Wall (Siegfried Line)—a 300-mile-long fortified defense line on Germany's western border. Eisenhower planned to rest and refurbish his armies during the winter (the coldest in 40 years) and prepare for the final fight for Germany and the big push toward Berlin. However, the Battle of the Bulge, Hitler's last-ditch offensive in the Ardennes (December 16, 1944, to January 28, 1945), temporarily disrupted Eisenhower's plans for a calm winter. But Hitler's big gamble failed.

Allied forces crossed the Rhine in March 1945 and swept with lightning speed across Germany. The Germans considered Patton to be their gravest threat, as one captured German officer indicated: "General Patton was always the main topic of military discussion. Where is he? When will he attack? Where? . . . How? With what? . . . [He was] the most feared general on all fronts." Hitler's armies began collapsing in the west and in the east. American and Soviet troops finally met at the Elbe River on April 25. The war in Europe ended with Germany's unconditional surrender on May 7, 1945. None of this would have been possible had it not been for the sacrifices and devotion to duty of all those who fought on the beaches and in the hedgerows of Normandy.

Eisenhower's men achieved a splendid victory in what he termed a "crusade in Europe" and President Franklin D. Roosevelt characterized as "a mighty endeavor." But what if history had witnessed a different scenario at Normandy? What if the Germans had thrown the Allies off the beaches and forced the invasion armada to return to England? What might have happened had Eisenhower and his men failed at Normandy? The alternatives range from adverse to catastrophic. A brief review of the most relevant "what ifs" might begin with the weather.

What if RAF group captain John M. Stagg had erred in his forecast for 36 hours of favorable weather commencing on the afternoon of June 5? Or what if Eisenhower had opted not to risk everything on that narrow window of opportunity? And what if the storm had continued after Ike had decided to set his forces in motion?

Eisenhower could have called back the invasion fleet, but to do so would have cost him the all-important element of surprise achieved through the FORTITUDE campaign and Patton's phantom army (FUSAG). Moreover, he would have revealed the Allied landing site. And had the storm struck after the landings began, he would have been forced to cancel the follow-on land-ings and to leave the men of the initial waves on the beaches to be killed or captured. An alternate scheduling held an even greater likelihood of failing, given that June 19—the date of the next suitable combination of full moon and low tides—yielded the year's worst storm in Normandy.

The opportunity for failure loomed so real in Eisenhower's mind at the time that between his decision to proceed and the start of the invasion he had prepared a so-called failure letter for release to the press. Its key sentences read: "The troops, the air and the Navy did all that bravery and devotion to duty could do. If any blame or fault attaches to the attempt it is mine alone."

Militarily, had the invasion failed, Eisenhower most certainly would have been relieved, leaving the Allies with a new commander—some say Patton—and no alternative strategy. The Allies had spent a year developing OVERLORD but not a single day on a backup plan. Politically, the British likely would have replaced Winston Churchill as prime minister, and the Americans probably would have elected Tom Dewey president in November 1944 instead of Franklin Roosevelt. Leadership changes result in policy changes.

Another attempt to land in Normandy would have been disastrous; the much stronger German defenses at the Pas de Calais defied an open attack without deception (which would no longer have been possible); and German fortifications at Le Havre discouraged even the boldest of the bold. Arguably, the only choice remaining to the Allies would have been to land in the south of France (as they did in Operation DRAGOON in mid-August 1944), but that would have entailed driving across all of France and Belgium to strike at Germany itself. Also, with the threat of a cross-Channel invasion removed—temporarily, at least—Hitler could draw reserves from the west to stem the Soviet tide in the east.

An Allied defeat at Normandy might have prolonged the war for several more years while the loss of life on both sides continued to mount. Meanwhile, the Germans were racing with the Americans to develop an atomic bomb. The Americans won the race, successfully testing the first atomic bomb in July 1945, two months after Germany's surrender. Had the Normandy invasion failed and the war dragged on, the United States might have decided to drop an atomic bomb on Germany, especially if the Germans had managed to defeat the Soviets. Fears that German scientists might be close to developing an atomic bomb would also have increased the pressure to launch a nuclear attack.

Had the Americans used atomic bombs on Germany, the armies of the western Allies still would have come together with the Soviet armies somewhere in central Europe. Whether they would have clashed or collaborated remains problematical. And had they clashed, would the United States have resolved the issue with the A-bomb? Who can say?

In another scenario, the Soviets might have defeated a weakened Germany and driven deep into western Europe, spreading communism as they went. (Allied bombing would have continued to deprive Germany of its production capacity and resources throughout this campaign.) It is not inconceivable that the entire Continent would have come under Soviet domination by the end of the war. With Germany smashed and Europe under his control, Stalin might then have turned his attention to the Far East, to Japan. At the very least, the Soviets might have succeeded in dividing Japan, as Korea was split after Japan's surrender in 1945. Had these events transpired, the Soviet Union might still exist—not only as a union of socialist states but also as the antagonist of the United States and its allies in a continuing cold war. And so long as the cold war continued, the ever-present threat of a nuclear war would diminish the quality of life around the globe.

Any of these imaginings and speculations—and more—*might* have happened but did not. They did not because Eisenhower and his men did not fail at Normandy.

■   ■   ■

Two decades after D Day, the former supreme commander at Normandy, who had gone on to become the 34th president of the United States, returned to Omaha Beach to honor the deeds of his former comrades in arms. In an interview with newsman Walter Cronkite, Dwight D. Eisenhower reflected on their sacrifices.

President George Bush dedicated the National D Day Memorial in Bedford, Virginia, on June 6, 2001, 57 years after the Allied invasion that was the turning point of World War II. Bedford was chosen to be the memorial site since 25 out of 35 soldiers sent from the small Virginia town to fight on D Day died. This is thought to be the highest per capita loss of any U.S. town.

"I think it's just overwhelming. To think of the lives that were given [to keep Hitler from destroying freedom in the world], paying a terrible price on this beach alone, on that one day, 2,000 casualties. But they did it so that the world could be free. It just shows what free men will do rather than be slaves."

1940

May 26–June 3	British and French troops evacuate Dunkirk
June 22	Fall of France
September 27	Germany, Italy, and Japan sign the Tripartite Pact

1941

June 2	Germany invades the Soviet Union
December 7	Japan attacks the U.S. naval base at Pearl Harbor
December 8	United States declares war on Japan
December 11	Germany and Italy declare war on the United States
December 22	Arcadia Conference, which runs until January 14, 1942, begins in Washington, D.C.

1942

April 1	President Franklin D. Roosevelt accepts the BOLERO invasion plan

December 8 ● United States declares war on Japan

● **December 11** Germany and Italy declare war on the United States

● **June 24** General Dwight D. Eisenhower arrives in Great Britain to assume command in the European theater

December 7 ● Japan attacks the U.S. naval base at Pearl Harbor

1941   **1942**

Timeline

June 24	General Dwight D. Eisenhower arrives in Great Britain to assume command in the European theater

1943

January 14–24	Casablanca Conference at Anfa (code-named SYMBOL)
March	Lieutenant General Sir Frederick E. Morgan is appointed Chief of Staff to the Supreme Allied Commander designate and begins planning for the Allied invasion of France
August 17–24	First Quebec conference (code-named QUADRANT)
November 28–December 1	Tehran Conference (code-named EUREKA)
December 24	General Dwight D. Eisenhower named Supreme Allied Commander

1944

February 14	Eisenhower names his principal subordinates
June 4	Eisenhower sets June 6 as D Day

March
Lieutenant General Sir Frederick E. Morgan appointed Chief of Staff to the Supreme Allied Commander designate and begins planning for the Allied invasion of France.

June 30
Operation Neptune ends

July 9
Caen falls to British and Canadian forces

June 27
U.S. 7th Corps captures Cherbourg

July 18
U.S. 29th Infantry Division enters St.-Lô

1943

1944

December 24
General Dwight D. Eisenhower named Supreme Allied Commander

June 4
Eisenhower sets June 6 as D Day

July 25–30
Operation Cobra

August 25
Normandy campaign ends

June 12
U.S. 7th Corps overruns Carentan

June 6
D Day; Operation Neptune commences

August 19
U.S. 79th Infantry Division crosses the Seine

June 5	Allied invasion fleet gathers in the English Channel
June 6	D Day; Operation NEPTUNE commences
June 7	Mulberries (artificial harbors) positioned off Omaha and Gold Beaches
June 12	U.S. 7th Corps overruns Carentan
June 19	Worst storm of the year strikes the English Channel, demolishing Mulberry at St. Laurent
June 27	U.S. 7th Corps captures Cherbourg
June 30	Operation NEPTUNE ends
July 7	Decisive battle for Caen commences
July 9	Caen falls to British and Canadian forces
July 17	Field Marshal Erwin Rommel is severely injured in car wreck after being strafed by British Spitfires
July 18	U.S. 29th Infantry Division enters St.-Lô
July 18–20	Operation GOODWOOD
July 25–30	Operation COBRA
August 1	Lieutenant General George S. Patton's U.S. 3rd Army is officially activated
August 19	U.S. 79th Infantry Division crosses the Seine
August 25	Normandy campaign ends
December 16	Battle of the Bulge begins

1945

January 28	Battle of the Bulge ends
April 25	American and Soviet troops meet at the Elbe River
May 7	Germany surrenders
May 8	VE Day

Ambrose, Stephen E. *Americans at War*. Jackson: University Press of Mississippi, 1997.

Badsey, Stephen. *Normandy 1944: Allied Landings and Breakout*. Campaign Series. General Editor David G. Chandler. Oxford, UK: Osprey Publishing, 1999.

Black, Robert W. *Rangers in World War II*. New York: Ballantine Books, 1992.

Brokaw, Tom. *The Greatest Generation*. New York: Random House, 1998.

Chandler, David G. *Battles and Battle Scenes of World War Two*. New York: Macmillan, 1989.

Chandler, David G., Colin McIntyre, and Michael C. Tagg. *Chronicles of World War II*. Godalming, UK: Bramley Books, 1997.

Chant, Christopher, ed. *Warfare and the Third Reich: The Rise and Fall of Hitler's Armed Forces*. New York: Smithmark, 1996.

Christman, Calvin L., ed. *America at War: An Anthology of Articles from MHQ: The Quarterly Journal of Military History*. Annapolis, Md.: Naval Institute Press, 1995.

Congdon, Don. *Combat World War II Europe: Unforgettable Eyewitness Accounts of the Momentous Military Struggles of World War II*. New York: Galahad Books, 1996.

Doubler, Michael D. *Closing with the Enemy: How GIs Fought the War in Europe, 1944–1945*. Lawrence: University Press of Kansas, 1994.

Dunnigan, James F., and Albert A. Nofi. *Dirty Little Secrets of World War II: Military Information No One Told You About the Greatest, Most Terrible War in History*. New York: William Morrow, 1994.

Flower, Desmond, and James Reeves, eds. *The War, 1939–1945: A Documentary History*. New York: Da Capo Press, 1997.

Gilbert, Martin. *The Second World War: A Complete History*. New York: Henry Holt, 1989.

Halliwell, Sarah, and Tim Cooke, eds. *Eyewitness War*. South Woodham Ferrers, UK: Publishing Corporation UK Ltd., 1995.

Hanson, Victor Davis. *The Soul of Battle: From Ancient Times to the Present Day, How Three Great Liberators Vanquished Tyranny*. New York: Free Press, 1999.

Hynes, Samuel. *The Soldiers' Tale: Bearing Witness to Modern War*. New York: Viking, 1997.

Jablonski, Edward. *A Pictorial History of the World War II Years*. New York: Wings Books, 1995.

Kilvert-Jones, Tim. *Omaha Beach: V Corps' Battle for the Normandy Beachhead*. Battleground Europe Series. Barnsley, UK: Leo Cooper/Pen & Sword Books, 1999.

Library of America. *Reporting World War II, Part Two: American Journalism 1944–1946*. New York: Library Classics of the United States, 1995.

Linderman, Gerald F. *The World Within War: America's Combat Experience in World War II*. New York: Free Press, 1997.

McCombs, Don, and Fred L. Worth, *World War II: 4,139 Strange and Fascinating Facts*. New York: Wings Books, 1996.

McManus, John C. *The Deadly Brotherhood: The American Combat Soldier in World War II*. Novato, Calif.: Presidio Press, 1998.

Messenger, Charles. *Sepp Dietrich: Hitler's Gladiator; the Life and Times of Oberstgruppenführer and Panzergeneral-Oberst der Waffen-SS Dietrich*. London: Brassey's, 1988.

Miller, David. *Great Battles of World War II: Major Operations That Affected the Course of the War*. New York: Crescent Books, 1998.

Miller, Robert A. *August 1944: The Campaign for France*. Novato, Calif.: Presidio Press, 1988.

Murphy, Edward F. *Heroes of World War II*. Novato, Calif.: Presidio Press, 1990.

O'Neill, William L. *A Democracy at War: America's Fight at Home and Abroad in World War II*. New York: Free Press, 1993.

Rice, Earle, Jr. *Strategic Battles in Europe*. American War Library Series. San Diego: Lucent Books, 2000.

Shilleto, Carl. *Utah Beach, St Mère Église*. Battleground Europe Series. Barnsley, UK: Leo Cooper/Pen & Sword Books, 2001.

Sulzberger, C. L. *World War II*. New York: American Heritage, 1985.

Taylor, A. J. P. *The Second World War and Its Aftermath*. London: Folio Society, 1998.

Terkel, Studs. *"The Good War": An Oral History of World War II*. New York: New Press, 1990.

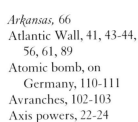

page:

2: Compass Projections
6: Associated Press, AP
9: Associated Press, AP
13: Hulton Archive by Getty Images
16: Associated Press, AP
18: Hulton Archive by Getty Images
21: Associated Press, AP
23: Hulton Archive by Getty Images
29: Compass Projections
33: Hulton Archive by Getty Images
35: Hulton Archive by Getty Images
36: Hulton Archive by Getty Images
38: Hulton Archive by Getty Images
40: Hulton Archive by Getty Images
41: Hulton Archive by Getty Images
45: Hulton Archive by Getty Images
50: Hulton Archive by Getty Images
52: Associated Press, AP

57: New York Public Library
61: Associated Press, AP
64: Hulton Archive by Getty Images
68: Associated Press, AP
75: National Archives
78: Hulton Archive by Getty Images
80: Hulton Archive by Getty Images
82: Associated Press, AP
88: Hulton Archive by Getty Images
91: Associated Press, AP
92: Associated Press, AP
94: Associated Press, AP
99: Associated Press, AP
102: Hulton Archive by Getty Images
104: Associated Press, AP
106: Hulton Archive by Getty Images
112: Associated Press, AP

cover: Franklin D. Roosevelt Library

EARLE RICE JR. is a former senior design engineer and technical writer in the aerospace industry. After serving nine years with the U.S. Marine Corps, he attended San Jose City College and Foothill College on the San Francisco Peninsula. He has devoted full time to his writing since 1993 and has written more than 30 books for young adults. Earle is a member of the Society of Children's Book Writers and Illustrators (SCBWI); the League of World War I Aviation Historians and its UK-based sister organization, Cross & Cockade International; the United States Naval Institute; and the Air Force Association.

VALLEY PARK COMMUNITY LIBRARY
320 Benton St.
Valley Park, MO 63088